CW01085413

YOUTH QUAKE 4.0

A WHOLE GENERATION AND THE NEW INDUSTRIAL REVOLUTION

Rocky Scopelliti

Marshall Cavendish
Business

Published by Marshall Cavendish Business
An imprint of Marshall Cavendish International

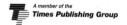
A member of the
Times Publishing Group

Other Marshall Cavendish Offices
Marshall Cavendish Corporation. 99 White Plains Road, Tarrytown NY 10591-9001,
USA • Marshall Cavendish International (Thailand) Co Ltd. 253 Asoke, 12th Flr,
Sukhumvit 21 Road, Klongtoey Nua, Wattana, Bangkok 10110, Thailand • Marshall
Cavendish (Malaysia) Sdn Bhd, Times Subang, Lot 46, Subang Hi-Tech Industrial
Park, Batu Tiga, 40000 Shah Alam, Selangor Darul Ehsan, Malaysia

Marshall Cavendish is a registered trademark of Times Publishing Limited

National Library Board, Singapore Cataloguing-in-Publication Data

Name(s): Scopelliti, Rocky, 1963-
Title: Youthquake 4.0 : a whole generation and the new industrial revolution /
Rocky Scopelliti.
Description: Singapore : Marshall Cavendish Business, 2018.
Identifier(s): OCN 1045423237 | ISBN 978-981-48-2861-1 (paperback)
Subject(s): LCSH: Generation Y--Attitudes. | Generation Y Employment. |
Generation Y--Social conditions. | Generation Y--Economic conditions.
Classification: DDC 305.2--dc23

Printed in Singapore

To my beloved family, late father and brother,
thank you for giving me this life.

To my friends who, in the face of my adversity,
awoke the stillness in my heart, thank you.

CONTENTS

INTRODUCTION

We are living in the age of accelerated transformation. While transformation itself is not necessarily new to us, the frequency, pace and impact of transformation today is unprecedented. There has never been a more important time to stop and consider the question: *How will we increase our capacity to adapt to a world of accelerated change?*

To answer this question, we will explore demographic change within the context of the environment that we can anticipate it will be exposed to. This is what we will examine in this book.

We know that populations are ageing, and that life expectancy has steadily been increasing by two to three years each decade. At the other end of the age spectrum, Millennials (18–34 years) have now become the largest demographic group on the planet, representing one in three (2.1 billion)[1] people. They are likely to be the first generation to have a 50 per cent chance of living to 100 years[2]. This means they are also likely to see the emergence of four-generation families, so our notion of family structure will profoundly change from what has come before. Their proportionate representation in society—whether it's as business leaders or policy makers in the workplace, government or institutions, or whether they are influencing spiritual, academic, scientific or technological advances—will only increase from here on. Millennials are integral to the question and the subject of this book.

Demographers Neil Howe and William Strauss invented the label 'Millennials', but this demographic cohort is also commonly referred to as Generation Y, those born between 1981–2000. Social researchers applied that label as it follows Generation X, or those born between 1965–1980. 'Baby Boomers' is the label used to describe those born between 1946–1964, most of whom are the parents of Millennials.

Millennials have become aware of the 100-year life and are planning accordingly.

From an environmental perspective, while the world's cities cover just two per cent of the Earth's surface, today they account for 55 per cent of its population[3]. Cities are predicted by the United Nations to be home to 86 per cent of global populations by 2050[4]. We are indeed *homo urbanis*.

These cities will become smarter as they, and our lives and businesses, become increasingly digitally connected. Until now these connected devices, sensors and systems have generated 90 per cent of the total data that has ever been produced[5]. Many analysts, however, predict that by 2020, some 200 billion objects will be connected—26 smart objects for every living person[6]. Just imagine what data will be produced and what new services and businesses these will give rise to by 2020?

Data has become the 21st century's energy, increasingly originating from urbanisation.

Intelligence is becoming predictive and artificially developed. Lifestyle processes and services are being automated. Healthcare quality and life expectancy is improving with advances in biotechnology, innovation and genetic engineering. Major threats to life, property and privacy are now digitally industrialised and borderless. Industries, organisations and ecosystems are regenerating or disappearing at exponential rates as they reprogram for the 21st century.

Life is anything but predictable and uncertainty has become the new normal as we transition into the imagination economy[7].

The convergence of demographically fuelled behavioural change associated with the Millennial demographic and emerging technologies associated with the Fourth Industrial Revolution are affecting every industry and every part of our global economy. The Fourth Industrial Revolution builds on the Third Technological Revolution and is characterised by the augmentation of technologies from the physical, digital and biological spheres[8].

Collectively, this convergence gives rise to an accelerated multiplication effect, which is why this book is titled

Youthquake 4.0. The impact of this effect is challenging our notions of how time is structured, innovation pursued, and how traditional models of production, distribution and scale are becoming decoupled from growth and the supply of scarce resources through exponential models.

It is worth reflecting that the First Industrial Revolution occurred from the 18th to 19th centuries, when mostly agrarian rural societies became industrial and urban. The development of the steam engine and textile industries were central to this revolution's development. The Second Industrial Revolution occurred between 1870 and 1914. This era saw the rise of steel, oil and electricity used to power and create mass production in assembly. Major technology advancements were in the areas of telecommunications, lighting, the phonograph and the internal combustion engine. The Third Industrial Revolution of the 1980s saw advancements in analogue through to digital technology, mechanical devices and automation. This period gave rise to the personal computer, the internet and information communication technology, including wireless technology, which is why it is also referred to as the Digital Revolution.

While our traditional linear view of the future, the models and methodologies we use to forecast and operate our businesses and the associated legacy technologies may have served us well in the First, Second and part of the Third Industrial Revolutions, they are inadequate and unreliable predictors of the future needs of societies, value creation, behaviour of markets, and economic performance or survival in the Fourth Industrial Revolution.

Welcome to 'Youthquake'—Oxford Dictionaries' 2017 word of the year

Youthquake is defined as a 'significant cultural, political, or social change arising from the actions or influence of young people'[9]. This is not a new term. Youthquake was first coined by *Vogue* magazine's editor-in-chief Diana Vreeland in 1965[10] to describe the cultural movement on the streets of London by a new generation of young people we now know as Baby Boomers. Vreeland wrote in her article entitled 'Youthquake':

Youth is surprising countries east and west with a sense of assurance serene beyond all years. First hit by the surprise wave, England and France already accept the new jump off age as one of the exhilarating realities of life today. The same exuberant tremor is now coursing through America, which practically invented this century's youth in the first place.

Ironically the term 'renaissance' five decades later has been used to describe Baby Boomers' children—the Millennials. We shouldn't be surprised that the first and most powerful influence on Millennials was their parents. Youthquake for Baby Boomers was so well captured in the lyrics 'There's a whole generation, With a new explanation, People in motion' in Scott McKenzie's 1967 hit song and generational anthem 'San Francisco (Be Sure to Wear Flowers in Your Hair)'[11]. That song reached number one in the United Kingdom, encapsulating the spirit of a generation during the 1960s craving significant cultural, political and social change.

An unusual generation? A problematic generation? A puzzling generation? A preoccupied generation? An entitled, ungrateful generation? Was there ever a rising generation in history *not* given those labels? As George Orwell so well articulated: 'each generation imagines itself to be more intelligent than the one that went before it, and wiser than the one that comes after it'.

Or are Millennials simply a generation that, like their Baby Boomer parents, have formed their social, cultural and economic beliefs from the environment in which they grew up? For example, might Millennials' perceived lack of loyalty reflect their perfectly understandable need to explore life's many options? Might their perceived entitlement be a misinterpretation of their empowerment? Might their preoccupation with technology reflect their desire to remain socially connected? The tsunami of stereotyping and typecasting directed at Millennials would seem to be over-generalizations born of misinterpretations, since they seem to have a clear idea about how to live in the contemporary world and they have a vision for its future. To them, the world is their neighborhood.

It is worth reflecting on one of the many essential points about their mostly Baby Boomer parents to help explain their influence on Millennials. In their view of the future, Baby Boomers were shaped by two different and contradictory influences.

First, Baby Boomers grew up in the postwar economic boom of the Second Industrial Revolution, where electric power was used to achieve mass production and the division of labour. There wasn't just a baby boom, but manufacturing, mining and housing booms. That period also saw the rise to power of the working class. Baby Boomers were enveloped in prosperity, developing an unquenchable thirst for in-home appliances, telephones fixed to walls, white goods, televisions, motor vehicles and leisure activities that fueled the creation of many new consumer markets.

The era ushered in suburbia. New neighbourhoods sprang up and the locality symbolized status, class and lifestyles. To Baby Boomers, life was a never-ending pathway of gratification, with the promise of success, wealth and opulence.

But this was tempered by the threat of no future at all.

The second powerful but contrasting influence on them was the Cold War. They grew up in the era of mutually assured destruction (MAD). This was the era of nuclear weapons being massively stockpiled by the United States and the Soviet Union, and the threat they would be used, triggering World War III. Baby Boomers grew up amidst this superpower tension.

So how did they reconcile these contradictory influences? Their motivation shifted from delayed gratification, to embracing *instant* gratification, despite this description being synonymous with Millennials. Baby Boomers' generational catch-cry was 'We're not here for a long time; we're here for a good time.' They became famous for their impatience—rushing into marriage, rushing into parenthood, rushing into debt—for their frivolous spending, and for their reluctance to plan for the long term.

Baby Boomers were labelled the 'Me Generation' by their parents—the 'Silent Generation' born between 1927–1945—who were puzzled by their self-indulgent, live-for-now mentality and liberated sexuality brought about by the contraceptive pill. But Baby Boomers were living in a way that was consistent with those contradictory influences.

As history now records, Baby Boomers were thankfully here for a long time. The good times of the 1960s were not fulfilled by the events of the 70s, 80s and 90s. Life was much harder for the Baby Boomers than they envisaged.

They were living through a 'Youthquake' that was characterised by transformations such as the gender revolution, which reshaped our views on marriage and divorce and redefined the nature of family life. Economies were restructured, including a radical redistribution of work and wealth between classes; there were levels of unemployment not seen since the Great Depression; and there was the beginning of the information technology revolution. While Baby Boomers were living the dream of retiring at 55, changes to the retirement age in many countries, a lack of planning, and the global financial crisis has seen most continue working for longer to achieve financial security in retirement.

Youthquake for Millennials, on the other hand, will be quite different to that of their parents. They traverse three distinct life stages. Stage one is the shift from youth to adulthood. For most, this occurs around the 17–18 year mark. Importantly, Millennials' participation in education is the highest of any generation. Among OECD countries, 42 per cent of Millennials aged 25–34 years hold a higher education degree, compared to 26 per cent of their Baby Boomer parents[12], and so this stage is very different to that of their parents.

Stage two, the transition from student life into professional life that occurs broadly between the ages of 18 to mid-20s, sees many Millennials graduating with a student debt, something that didn't exist for their parents. Stage three, the transition from single life into family life, sees many Millennials, unlike their Baby Boomer parents, staying single for longer. For example, in the United States, 48 per cent of Baby Boomers were married by the age of 32, versus 26 per cent of Millennials[13].

While these stages are being deferred for longer compared to their Baby Boomer parents, as each of these transitions occur, their needs, expectations, economic value and attitudes toward life fundamentally change. Why is it, then, that they continue to be typecast as though they are the same globally? It doesn't make sense, right? We need to smash the 'smashed avocado on toast' stereotype, because Millennials have grown up in a different environment to other generations.

Millennials grew up during the Digital Revolution that began in the 1980s, where the advancement of technology saw the shift from mechanical and analogue electronic technology to digital electronics. Amidst that information technology environment, they developed into the most highly-educated, diverse, media-saturated and connected generation. They are now shaping the 21st century and will propel the Fourth Industrial Revolution.

To Millennials, their voice and influence is global through the social media they continue to fuel. It's instantly delivered to their smartphones, and that's become as natural to them as the air they breathe, efficiently consumed through the artificially intelligent, personalised, platform-based, exponential models serving them. We need to embrace them, not ostracise them. We need to go beyond just listening to them as they crave to be heard. For this generation, their catch cry will be: 'We're here for a good time and we're here for a long time, so we'd better take care of our world.'

Just like their parents, who gave rise to the *economic boom*, this generation will give rise to the next *technological boom*.

Welcome also to the *Fourth Industrial Revolution* that is augmenting our physical, digital and biological systems

As Klaus Schwab, founder and executive chairman of the World Economic Forum describes: 'we are at the beginning of a revolution that is fundamentally changing the way we live, work and relate to one another'. He also proposes that 'businesses, industries and corporations will face continuous Darwinian pressure and as such, the philosophy of "always in beta" always evolving will become more prevalent'[14].

This philosophy directly informs the question at hand; in this environment, how do we increase our capacity to adapt? The evidence to date suggests that nations, industries and corporations are yet to fully capitalise on the benefits of the current digital revolution, which may well be the single biggest barrier to unlocking the potential of the Fourth Industrial Revolution.

This revolution is characterised by emerging technology breakthroughs with potentially highly disruptive effects in the areas of artificial intelligence, robotics, the Internet of Things (IoT), autonomous vehicles, 3D printing, biotechnology, nanotechnology, materials science, energy storage, blockchain and quantum computing. Mastering the Fourth Industrial Revolution was the theme of the World Economic Forum Annual Meeting in 2016 in Davos-Klosters, Switzerland. According to Klaus Schwab, the Fourth Industrial Revolution differs from the previous ones in its speed, scale and impact.

It will be a cyber-physical system characterised by new technologies that are augmenting our digital, physical and biological worlds. In this book I will argue that 'interconnected trust' is what fuses those worlds, requiring a paradigm shift in relationships between ideas, people and technology—and, as such, is a further reason why this revolution differs from those in the past.

Why write this book?

As 2017 drew to a close, I was saddened by the illnesses impacting my family and friends. I couldn't wait for the year to end. Serendipitously, it was announced that the term 'Youthquake' was the Oxford Dictionaries Word of the Year 2017. The word not only reflected the ethos, mood and preoccupations of 2017, but was also judged as having lasting potential as a word of cultural significance. My sadness immediately dissipated, replaced by an overwhelming sense of joy and happiness. Yes, I thought, the world finally gets that it's *their* (Millennials) time, and this juvenescence is a singularity for us all to embrace and celebrate.

As heartbreaking as it is witnessing loved ones' lives evaporating, it's important and joyous to imagine what life can be. My life's purpose is to make the world a better place through thought leadership and those personal experiences presented me, in that moment, the gift of Youthquake. As an ambassador of this amazing Millennial generation, this was just the best news. Thoughts of Youthquake, then, became my happiness sanctuary.

Through this book I will explain how this remarkable generation, equipped with the most exciting technological advancements of the Fourth Industrial Revolution, will impact all facets of our society, making our world a better place.

For many years, I've been privileged to research how Millennials and digital technology are impacting our world. Importantly, we have now crossed two major inextricably linked inflection points that require new thinking and leadership about human and technological adaptation. The Millennial demographic has now become the largest demographic on the planet and a global phenomenon, together with next-generation technologies, in shaping humanity with the Fourth Industrial Revolution.

I'm often surprised by the number of organisations that report they are 'customer centric', 'employees are engaged', 'stakeholders consulted', 'investor aligned' and 'technologically transformed'— yet what's missing is an integrated strategy that puts a 'face' to those customers, employees, policy makers, partners and investors. If it's about customer acquisition, 'well that's marketing's area'; if it's about employment, 'well that's human resources' area'; if it's about innovation, 'well that's digital's or IT's area'. Millennials are treated as though they have multiple lives, but they are the same people, they just don't compartmentalise their lives like previous generations; they expect their lives to be intertwined.

I'm equally intrigued by the simultaneous fascination and anxiety that leaders have around disruption, innovation, and transformation, and the treatment of these forces as though they are mutually exclusive from human capital and demographic change. Digital is often referred to as a contemporary descriptor for the IT department. Or what marketing and sales does to attract and sell to customers. Or what operations does to improve productivity or efficiency. What's missing is a wholistic view and strategy about what digital means to their customers, employees, business model, the industry ecosystem within which they function, and what this means to their organisation's purpose.

The globalisation of disruption shows no signs of abating. The investment environment is awash with capital and has developed an unquenchable thirst for entrepreneurship. Global annual venture capital funding surged 50 per cent in 2017 to US$164 billion invested across 11,042 deals, propelled by Asia now representing 43 per cent of that investment, United States 44 per cent, and Europe 11 per cent[15]. Start-ups, accelerator programs and innovation hubs are now globally thriving from locations in Silicon Valley, New York, London, Israel, China, Sydney, Berlin, Singapore, etc. Whichever way you look at disruption, the numbers are staggering. And while studies show that age is not a predictor of the success of start-ups, the Millennial generation has had more access to capital and resources, as well as the desire and skills, than the generations preceding them—which is demonstrated by the capacity that investors, corporates and governments have created by investing in their ideas and initiatives.

These forces are not mutually exclusive, but rather symbiotic.

This book aims to be the *Desiderata* of how the Millennials and the Fourth Industrial Revolution collectively influence the way we think about our social, cultural, economic and technological future: 'a whole generation, with a new industrial revolution and they are both in motion'. I will analyse the confluence of these two inextricably linked global forces, leveraging research from world-leading institutions and thought leaders to provide insights toward global challenges, economics, society, technology and innovation. It will transform the way you think about this remarkable generation and the influence they will increasingly have. It will invoke excitement for the unimaginable innovation that awaits us in the Fourth Industrial Revolution and the numerous resulting opportunities for citizens, societies and businesses.

The insights in this book are for individuals, leaders and policymakers seeking to unlock opportunities by developing specific adaption or transformation strategies from the interplay between the Millennial mind and the emerging technologies in the Fourth Industrial Revolution. Importantly, I hope these insights inspire you to consider the role you can play in adapting your organisation's immune system, which today may be resisting change. For individuals, the pursuit of making the world a better place might be one of your most rewarding life experiences. Organisations that reinvent themselves effectively will become the beneficiaries of the future sources of leadership, skills, entrepreneurship, corporate social responsibility, innovation and resulting profits.

YOUTH QUAKE 4.0

WELCOME TO YOUTHQUAKE

Chapter One

DEMOGRAPHIC INFLUENCE

Millennials aren't entitled; they're empowered

> *The future promise of any nation can be directly*
> *measured by the present prospects of its youth.*

— John F. Kennedy
35th President of the United States

I'm sure most of us can recall where we were when major events occur in the world. For me, 24 June 2016 is a date I'll always remember. After a 22-hour flight from Sydney to London, my family and I were somewhat fatigued, but eager to experience the first leg of a wonderful three-week holiday in Europe. I was excited to witness my children's first classic English experience—the black cab at Heathrow airport. I had elevated my children's expectations about these iconic vehicles and the extensive training English taxi drivers undertake to perform their job.

'Covent Garden, thanks driver,' I said, followed by 'This is my kids' first trip to Europe and I'm sure they'd love to know what they can expect this week in London?' The driver replied disappointedly, 'We're no longer part of Europe. Yesterday was

Brexit day and it's going to be a gloomy week.' He then shared with us for the 45-minute drive into London how this was a tragic day in English and European history. What caught my attention in the driver's comments was how disappointed he was in the result, given that pre-polling indicating that 73 per cent of young people wanted to remain part of the European Union (EU). 'They didn't vote,' he said. His point was that Millennials did not participate in the referendum to the extent they could have, and if they had, the result would have been completely different, given the narrow margin of victory. When we got out of the taxi, my daughter said to me, 'Gee, English taxi drivers know a lot about politics too, don't they?'

That first day in London was quite surreal, as was that week, as predicted by that taxi driver. Commentators, bus drivers, politicians, business leaders and the British public were asking questions: How did this happen? What does it mean? Who do we blame or thank? Exit polls reported that older voters favoured exiting the EU and younger voters favoured remaining in the EU. The 'Remain' supporters looked on in despair, stunned and bewildered by the result. A student from Staffordshire University interviewed by BBC News[16] said: 'I'm annoyed that Baby Boomers have messed things up for us again.' Had a generational divide opened up in the UK, I wondered? And is this divide global?

Let's begin by considering some very significant statistical demographic changes occurring throughout the world, how they may impact society, and the policy dilemmas and opportunities they present for politicians and business leaders.

First, the ageing population. The increasing proportion of older persons in a population is poised to become one of the most significant global social transformations of the 21st century. According to the United Nations[17], between 2015 and 2030 the number of people in the world aged 60 years or over is projected to grow by 56 per cent, from 901 million to 1.4 billion. Between 2015 and 2050, when today's Millennials reach 60 years of age, the global population of older persons is projected to double to nearly 2.1 billion. The number of people aged 80 years or over, the 'oldest old persons', is growing even faster, and the United Nations predicts it will almost triple between 2018 and 2050 to 434 million (see Figures 1, 2 and 3).

This massive ageing trend has implications for nearly all sectors of society, including labour markets, financial markets, and the demand for goods and services, such as housing, transportation and social support, as well as family structures and their intergenerational ties.

Second, 2015 was a landmark year demographically, with Millennials between the ages of 18–35 years rising to become the most populous age group on the planet. Almost one in three humans are part of a Millennial population that numbers more than two billion people (see Figure 4). By 2050, they'll be 54–69 years old and will occupy positions of leadership across government, businesses, religious institutions and broader society.

As a result, Millennials have now become a leading indicator for social, political, economic, cultural and technological

Figure 1: World Population 2018

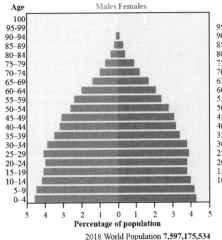

2018 World Population **7,597,175,534**
Source: Population Pyramid.
Reproduced by permission.

Figure 2: World Population 2030

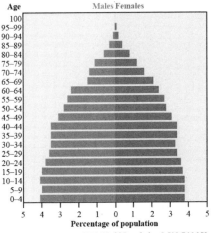

2030 World Population **8,500,766,052**
Source: Population Pyramid.
Reproduced by permission.

Figure 3: World Population 2050

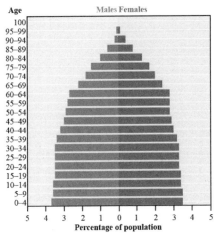

2050 World Population **9,725,147,993**
Source: Population Pyramid.
Reproduced by permission.

Figure 4: World Population by generational group 2015

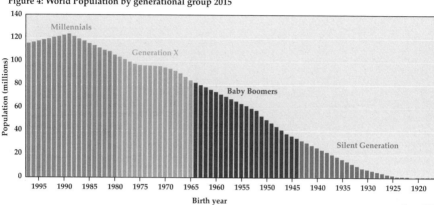

Source: UN

development. For political parties, their global voice will increasingly influence policy direction. For businesses, their value will influence economic performance. For employers, their technological proficiency will see the adoption of emerging disruptive technologies that fundamentally change our world at rates and scales of unprecedented levels. For society, their values and beliefs will influence our cultures.

So, let's consider the concentration of Millennials by country. Most of them, i.e. 86 per cent, live in large emerging markets[18], with half from Brazil, India, China and Indonesia[19]. These countries are also the most heavily populated. We can also see that at a regional level Asia has become the 'Millennial epicentre', where 58 per cent of Millennials live (see Figure 5).

The scale of Millennials in those countries' populations provides the opportunity for economic growth through what the International Monetary Fund describes as the 'demographic dividend'. This is achieved in two ways. Through investment in economic development and family welfare leading to growth in per capita income; and through the accumulation of assets that become invested domestically, or internationally, resulting in rising national income.

Figure 5: Global Millennial concentration by country and region 2015

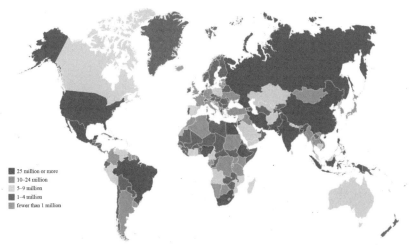

Source: UN World Population Prospects 2015; A.T. Kearney analysis

In developing countries such as Bangladesh, the Philippines and Vietnam, this means that deploying their vast Millennial populations could lead to rapid growth projected to be 6 per cent of GDP by 2020. In contrast, in some countries where unemployment is relatively high, such as Egypt (42 per cent), Iran (29 per cent) and South Africa (53 per cent), we see lower than average projected GDP growth (2–4 per cent) out to 2020, reflecting undercapitalization on the potential demographic dividend from their vast Millennial populations.

In developed countries and regions such as the United States, the United Kingdom, Australia, New Zealand, Japan and western Europe, lower fertility rates over many decades have led to relatively lower concentrations of Millennials in those populations. However, as we discussed earlier in this chapter, with ageing populations, and particularly Baby Boomers at the lower end of the age bracket now reaching retirement age, Millennials in many of those developing countries are rapidly becoming a larger part of the workforce.

As outlined earlier, according to projections by the United Nations[20], the number of older persons globally is growing faster than for any other age group. In contrast, over the same period, the number of people 24 years old or younger will grow a mere 11 per cent and the number of people aged 25–59 years will grow by 62 per cent. These projections underline the significant representation Millennials will continue to have through to 2050 as those born around 1980 reach 70 years of age. Importantly, with increased life expectancy, their democratic influence will continue to be felt.

In democracies, collectively the 'Youthquakers' (Millennials and Baby Boomers) have massive voting power to shape and influence policy. However, satisfying the economic and social demands of these very diverse groups is a major challenge for governments and political parties.

We are starting to see evidence of this demographic shift on the political stage. In the UK, Millennials make up approximately

31 per cent of the population. In the 2017 British general election, the greatest increase in voter turnout was among those aged between 18–34, reportedly a 16 point increase compared to any other demographic group (see Figure 6). Jeremy Corbyn's Labour Party was the primary beneficiary of this surge in participation.

In the United States, in 2016, the estimated 62 million Millennials had overtaken Generation X and the Silent Generation to become the second largest influential voting demographic group (see Figure 7). As the Baby Boomer voting-eligibility population continues to decline from its peak in 2004, the eligible Millennial vote will continue to rise through immigration and naturalization and they will become the largest voting demographic in the US.

Figure 6: Britain voter turnout 2017 general elections by age (%)

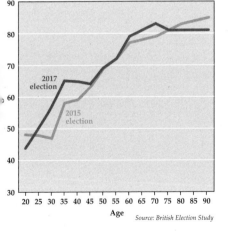

Source: British Election Study

Figure 7: Number of USA Millennials (20–35 years) eligible to vote by generation (1996–2016 election)

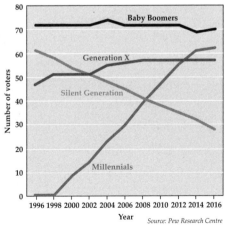

Source: Pew Research Centre

Empowerment

How will Millennials change the world?

The answer, I suspect, will be based on empowerment. History is filled with examples of how empowered individuals, cultures, communities or nations have inspired profound change—such as the post-World War II economic boom, the social and cultural changes of the 1960s, and the technology revolution of the 1980s. Empowered people and societies can be found underpinning each of them. So it is important that we explore what empowers Millennials, and how they will exercise this empowerment.

In its Annual 2017 Global Shapers Survey[21] of 31,495 people aged 18–35 across 186 countries, the World Economic Forum identified Millennials' attitudes, views and values toward a range of key global developments and challenges. One of those was empowerment.

The Third Industrial Revolution not only provided Millennials with universal access to the internet, it created a plethora of new, often decentralised, ways they could express their values, creativity and entrepreneurship. This they rate as the most important factor with youth empowerment (see Figure 8).

One of the most interesting questions in technology right now is about centralization vs decentralization. A lot of us got into technology because we believe it can be a decentralizing force that puts more power in people's hands.

— **Mark Zuckerberg**
founder Facebook

Figure 8: What are the most important factors contributing to youth empowerment in your country? (N=22,493)

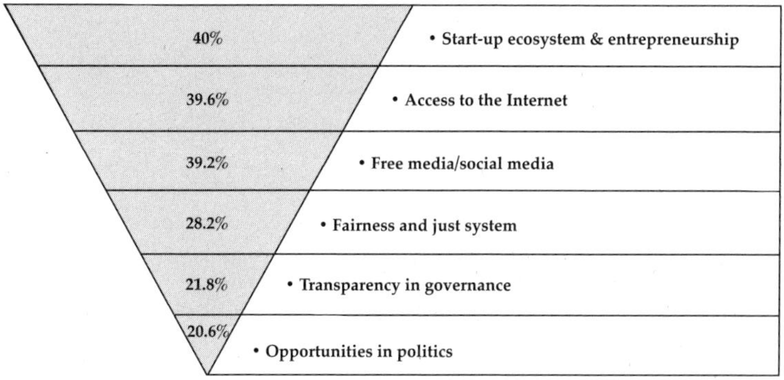

40%	• Start-up ecosystem & entrepreneurship
39.6%	• Access to the Internet
39.2%	• Free media/social media
28.2%	• Fairness and just system
21.8%	• Transparency in governance
20.6%	• Opportunities in politics

Data Source: World Economic Forum

This decentralization allowed Millennials to become more engaged with the world around them, and more socially conscious, economically considered and environmentally informed. An entrepreneurial spirit, connection via the internet and the media it enables (both free and social), are the pillars of empowerment. Importantly, it gives them the means to gather information to define the values that matter to them and a platform to expound those values. Connectivity through technology has empowered this generation to link instantly to the world around them.

This desire is not unique to Millennials. All generations have hungered to connect to the communities that matter to them. What's different today is that technology has enabled Millennials to connect instantly and on a global scale. This is why we are seeing social, political, economic and other issues challenged at a global scale and in real-time. Their empowerment may explain why they are more attracted to experiences and subscription model services rather than ownership, like their Baby Boomer parents.

Interestingly, empowerment isn't viewed by Millennials as an individual pursuit. To them it also includes empowering others to succeed. This strikes at the heart of their expectations of leaders, whether political, business, spiritual, or organisational. As we will explore in the following chapters, these expectations are falling short of the mark on matters of trust, and the role of business and the workplace. I'll close this chapter with a message from a songwriter who has become a worldwide success thanks . to the support of Millennials.

I believe that every single one of us, celebrity or not, has a responsibility to get involved in trying to make a difference to the world. Our generation faces many challenges, some of which were passed down to us by past generations, but it's up to us to find solutions today so that we don't keep passing our problems on.

— Shakira
singer-songwriter

Chapter summary

- Both demographic change associated with Millennials and technological change associated with the Fourth Industrial Revolution are affecting every industry and every part of the global economy.

- Millennials are the children of Baby Boomers, another very disruptive generation, who are the former's first and most significant influence.

- Just like their parents who gave rise to the economic boom, Millennials will give rise to the next technological boom—the Fourth Industrial Revolution.

- The concentration of Millennials in a country's population has become a lead indicator of social direction, policy and economic performance.

- Emerging markets are home to 86 per cent of Millennials. China is a great example of what other developing markets can achieve when leveraging this demographic.

- Capitalising on the significant representation of Millennials in a population can give a country a demographic dividend leading to economic growth.

- The internet has empowered Millennials and their global voice will be felt through creativity and entrepreneurship.

- With declining birth rates from generations preceding Millennials, ageing populations will have global implications and their presence will be felt for a very long time.

- This empowered generation is more attracted to experiences and subscription to services rather than physical ownership. To them, empowerment extends to 'empowering others to succeed', which is their expectation of today's leaders. The reality of this expectation is falling short of the mark.

Chapter Two

ECONOMIC INFLUENCE

Millennials vote with their money, and over time, they'll have more of it

> *A bank is a place that will lend you money,*
> *if you can prove that you don't need it.*

> **— Bob Hope**
> *comedian, actor, singer, dancer and entertainer*

Fifteen years ago, I joined the Commonwealth Bank of Australia (CBA) and worked closely with both the internet banking and youth segment marketing teams as we developed the mobile banking and payments strategy for the bank. We considered how mobile technology would revolutionize the way people banked and, in particular, how the emerging Millennial demographic would have very different expectations about the world and their place in it.

Through CBA's heritage and ongoing commitment to financial literacy, the bank held the largest youth customer base of any organisation type in Australia and understood this point well. I recall other major organisations from other industries seeking the bank's insights on how they achieved success through its youth programs. Despite other banks targeting the youth market once they left school and became profitable, CBA invested heavily in financial inclusion and education programs at points where customer profitability was questionable. With my commercial hat on, I asked why the bank invested in attracting unprofitable customers? The reply was, 'Because one day they will be profitable, and the loyalty we gain in investing in them now, will one day be returned to us in the form of profitable, loyal relationships.'

This was that moment that inspired my imagination, fascination, and obsession with Millennials. I saw how the convergence of behavioural change and digital technology with this demographic is going to economically disrupt the world in ways we've not seen with previous generations.

In this chapter I'll explore this generation's economic power in terms of income production capacity, investment capacity and spending power, and the impact and influence it will have.

Average economic value (AEV)

To understand the relative value of Millennials in a population versus the value of the total population in a country, I've created a measure that I'll refer to as average economic value (AEV). The AEV is an economic capacity measure defined as the total balance value of both funds in deposits and outstanding debt held with a financial institution expressed in US dollars. For this analysis, I've studied 6,078 Millennials in

15 countries across the Americas, Asia, Middle East and Europe (see Figure 9).

Averaged across those 15 countries, the AEV of Millennials has now reached 70 per cent of AEV across all age groups—meaning they are already a valuable generation.

Using this capacity measure, their value will only increase and their AEV will surpass that of other groups. We can expect Millennials' economic capacity to increase through time as they accumulate savings and increase debt. Debt, however, becomes a major issue. For Millennials, debt represents 41 per cent of their AEV, compared to 34 per cent for the total market average. Much of the economic value of Millennials is underpinned by debt.

Figure 9: Average Economic Value (AEV) – Millennials v Total Population (USD)

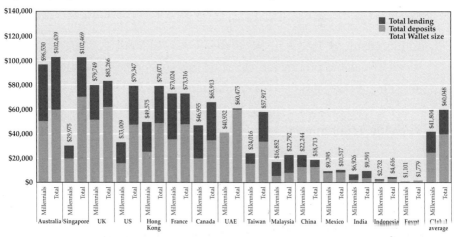

Source: RFi Intelligence
Reproduced by permission

At a country level, we see a wide distribution between Millennials AEV, compared to the respective averages across the total population. In some countries, Millennials' AEV has already overtaken the average of the total population. For example, in China, Millennials' AEV exceeds that of the total population by 22 per cent. However, a closer look reveals that Millennials in China have used debt to drive their AEV (42 per cent), when compared to the average debt across the total population (31 per cent).

The same profile exists in France, where Millennials have reached AEV parity with the average of the total population. However, 51 per cent of that AEV is made up of debt, compared to 35 per cent for the total population AEV.

In Australia and the United Kingdom, Millennials AEV are within five per cent of the total population AEV, making them a priority segment for organisations to target. As with France, for Australian and US Millennials, debt makes up about half (47 per cent and 50 per cent respectively) of their AEV, and less so for Millennials in the UK, where debt represents about 35 per cent of the AEV.

In Canada, although Millennials' AEV is 71 per cent of the total population AEV, they have the highest proportion of debt in their AEV (57 per cent) of the 15 countries studied. Millennials in Singapore, United Arab Emirates and Egypt carry significantly more deposits in their AEV mix and are less reliant on debt.

When we look at deposits, we can see that Millennials have reached 62 per cent of the average deposits held by the total population across the 15 countries studied. This contradicts the perception that Millennials are poor savers.

At a country level, Chinese Millennials hold more deposits than the average held across the total population. In Australia and the UK, Millennials have reached 84 per cent of the average deposits held by the total population. This reflects the growing importance of the economic value of Millennials in those countries.

The largest gaps between Millennials' average deposits compared to the average deposits of the total population are in Singapore where the gap is 71 per cent, followed by the United States where the gap is 66 per cent.

What we can conclude from looking at Millennials' AEV relative to the total population and across a wide range of countries is that their increasing economic capacity and its associated influence impacts the way we need to think about economic policy, financial markets and society. Millennials have come of economic age. Let's now unpack this AEV and consider the influences on both asset accumulation and liabilities.

Income production capacity

As discussed in Chapter One, as Millennials' proportionate representation increases, the first significant impact will be on workplaces. Millennials are estimated to represent 75 per cent of the workforce by 2025 in many countries. As this shift unfolds, their income production power is projected to increase to US$32 trillion by 2030[22]. As highlighted in Chapter One, Asia-Pacific will become a Millennial epicentre. Millennials are projected to be 58 per cent of the region's population, with disposable income estimated to be US$6 trillion[23]. By comparison, in the US, Millennials are predicted to become the primary producer of income by 2025, generating an estimated US$8.3 trillion (see Figure 10).

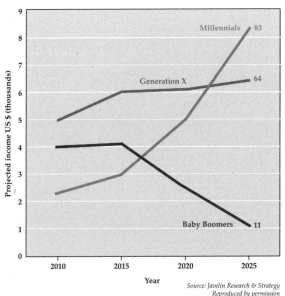

Figure 10: Projected US income by generation to 2025E (USD)

Source: Javelin Research & Strategy
Reproduced by permission

This inflection point will significantly influence global economies and markets as Millennials exercise their own preference for the allocation of discretionary and non-discretionary spending change—a point I'll return to.

Investment capacity

When it comes to Millennials' wealth, there are two things to consider. First, what they currently hold and what wealth they are likely to generate organically. Second, what wealth they stand to acquire through inheritance or intergenerational wealth transfer over time. According to the Boston Consulting Group's analysis[24] in 2015, Millennials held 10 per cent of the world's wealth estimated to be US$16.9 trillion, which they predict to double to an estimated US$35.3 trillion by 2020. The geographic distribution of that Millennial wealth is interesting. At a regional level, Millennial wealth in the Asia-Pacific (excluding Japan) already exceeds that of other regions, reflecting the rise of Asian economies and the region's high Millennial representation (see Figure 11).

Figure 11: Share of Millennials-controlled wealth by market/region 2015 (per cent)

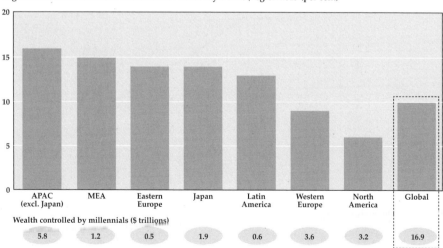

Source: BCG
Reproduced by permission

The way this wealth is managed has caught the attention of entrepreneurs and today is the subject of major disruption. This empowered generation desires 'self-direction' when it comes to wealth management. This desire for self-direction is manifesting as the rise of automated digital advice—often driven by Artificial Intelligence—commonly referred to as 'robo-advice'. Research indicates that Millennials place greater trust in technology-enabled advice than that of human originated advice—something I'll examine in more detail in Chapter Five.

We can also see the desire for self-direction playing out in the exponential growth of funds under disruptive wealth management platform players, such as WealthPoint and Betterment. They have emerged as two of the largest robo-advisers and have collectively raised US$405 million in aggregate funding to 2017. Nearly a decade after they launched, WealthPoint and Betterment collectively manage approximately $15.9 billion of assets for over 495,000 client accounts[25]. That's nearly one per cent of the total wealth that Millennials held in 2015. Now before you think that's not much, remember that these two organisations barely existed a decade ago.

Interestingly, we can see the exponential impact of these two platforms when we consider the explosive customer growth of these organisations since 2014. I'll cover the topic of exponential performance in more detail in Chapter Eight.

As Millennials assume a greater share of wealth, we can expect this empowered, self-directed, socially conscious generation to think quite differently about how and where their assets are allocated. The emergence of socially responsible asset classes is likely a lead indicator of this change. Impact investing is a rapidly growing segment of wealth management and sustainable investment assets grew to US$22.89 trillion globally in 2016, up 25 per cent from 2014[26]. Millennials are twice as likely to make sustainable investments than the average investor. Seventy-five per cent believe that their investments can influence change in social issues, climate change and gun control. Millennials think quite differently about who they trust to be their wealth custodians.

Student debt

Millennials are the most highly-educated generation ever, with 42 per cent of 25–34 years among OECD countries holding a higher education degree compared to 26 per cent of their Baby Boomer parents (see Figure 12).

Figure 12: Population with tertiary education 2016

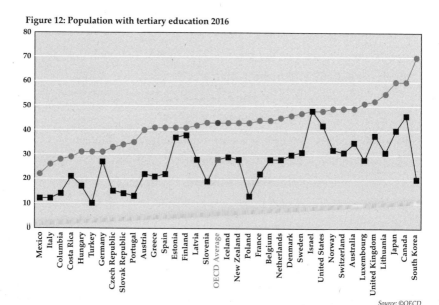

Source: ©OECD

This has come at a significant cost in many countries. Prolonged education is creating shifts in life stages (which I examine in Chapter Seven). It is also creating economic challenges for governments, with Millennials beginning their careers with huge levels of debt. The average student loan debt in 2016 was US$37,000 in the United States, US$55,000 in the United Kingdom[27] and AU$29,850 in Australia. In the United States, the student debt burden has tripled to US$1.4 trillion in the 10 years to 2016. In the United Kingdom, student debt has doubled to £100 billion over five years. In Australia, student debt has risen to AUD$59.7 billion[28].

In many countries, Millennials are the first generation to carry significant student debt. In the US, 2008–2009 was the inflection point where student loan debt overtook auto loan debt. Today student debt exceeds auto loan debt by US$1.1 trillion[29].

This presents one of the most significant opportunities for organisations competing to attract and retain Millennial workforces—financing their education. While these structures aren't yet widely available, they are on the rise. Structures vary from tax effective repayment arrangements through to full repayment by the employer once tenure commitments are completed. Organisations using this approach cover a wide range of industries including: Aetna (healthcare), Credit Suisse (global financial services), Fidelity Investments (financial services) and PricewaterhouseCoopers (global professional services).

If unaddressed, the rising costs and growing debt could affect economies, with the consequences including delayed marriage, home ownership and families and limited disposable income. A rethink of policy and collaboration is required in both the education and private sectors for skills in a rapidly changing world.

Spending capacity

Countries with high concentrations of Millennials are good early lead indicators for observing economic change. For example, in China, approximately 415 million Millennials make up 31 per cent of the population[30]. The explosive take-up of smartphones by Millennials reaching approximately 90 per cent penetration, has driven an unquenchable thirst in e-commerce and mobile payments. Approximately 73 per cent of online Chinese shoppers use mobile payments. In the United States, Millennials make up 31 per cent of the population—or approximately 80 million people[31]—and smartphone penetration among them has reached 97 per cent[32]. Approximately 80 per cent of US Millennials use banking apps[33].

Let's examine spending capacity through the lens of US credit card data. Analysing data collected over a year by Bank of America Merrill Lynch in 2017, we find some interesting patterns. First, each of the four demographic groups spends approximately 41–45 per cent of their income on one of the primary essentials: food. However, Millennials spend more on restaurants rather than groceries (52 per cent of income, as compared to 41 per cent for Generation X, 33 per cent for Baby Boomers and 33 per cent for Traditionalists).

Second, Millennials spend more on lifestyle items such as electronics/hobbies/clothing than older demographics (2–7 per cent)[34]. When it comes to lifestyles, delayed life stages from student life to professional life, and from single life to family life, indicate differences between this demographic and previous generations. (I will examine this in more detail in Chapter Seven.)

US Millennials carry fewer credit cards than older demographics. According to Experian, they carry lower balances than Baby Boomers (US$4,315 versus US$7,550)[35]. Student debt and a 'credit conservatism' arising from their experiences of the Global Financial Crisis may provide an explanation for lower use of credit than older demographics.

However, Experian found that while they tend to hold less credit balances on credit cards, they carry that balance forward significantly longer than older demographics (Millennials show a 36 per cent utilisation ratio versus Baby Boomers' 28 per cent), indicating they use (and rely upon) a higher percentage of the total available credit than Baby Boomers.

While the value of Millennials spending-power is influenced by many factors, their increasing representation in the workforce and subsequent income production, together with shifts in professional and family structures, will see them eventually overtake other generations in terms of their value. This is illustrated in a generational Portfolio Profitability Model[36] that uses US card portfolios and card profitability to predict this generational shift. It depicts declining profit (legacy) from the

Figure 13: Peak and legacy profits population over time (by generation per cent)

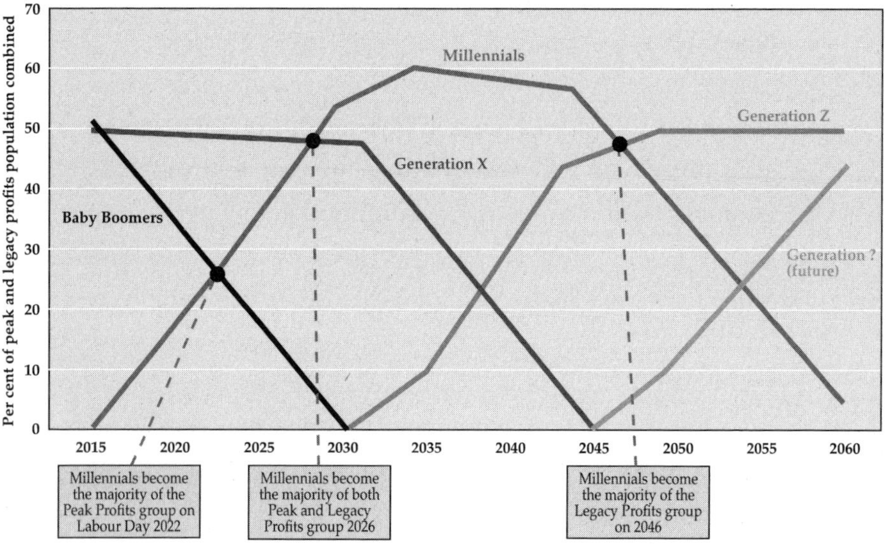

Source: ISYS analysis of the US Census Bureau population projections released December 2014
Reproduced by permission

Baby Boomers and Generation X, with a proportionate increase in the peak profit contribution from Millennials (see Figure 13).

The model predicts that Millennials will overtake Baby Boomers by 2022 and Generation X by 2028 to become the primary producer of profit, a position they are predicted to hold for 18 years, at which point they'll be overtaken by Generation Z. While we can reliably predict the spending power of this generation, how they will spend their money is much less certain as they transition into mobile-first experiences and a predominance of consumption-based or access-based services rather than ownership of them.

So, what influences their financial security?

According to a UBS study of affluent Millennials across 10 countries[37], whether they are from developed markets or emerging markets, when it comes to their financial security, Millennials were found to place high importance on their personal abilities in the areas of education and flexibility. UBS further found that technology skills and ambition ranked high in these priorities. When it comes to societal factors, Millennials reported the job market, social networks, economic policy and family responsibilities highest.

Millennial economics will be unlike previous generations across the production and accumulation phases, because the environment in which they live is profoundly changing. I'll examine this changing environment throughout the rest of this book. The most significant point to consider is Millennials' rapidly changing preferences. These preferences have been significantly shaped by the Technology Revolution. This demographic, more so than others before them, understands how to exert their economic influence on policy—be that social, economic, political or cultural.

Dogs have no money. Isn't that amazing? They're broke their entire lives. But they get through. You know why dogs have no money? No Pockets.

— Jerry Seinfeld
comedian, actor, writer, producer and director

Chapter summary

- Millennials average economic value (AEV) (balance values of deposit + lending), has reached 70 per cent of the AEV across 15 countries, which makes them an economically significant demographic.

- Millennials are much more reliant on debt, which has inflated the size of their AEV, representing 41 per cent, compared to 34 per cent of the total market average.

- As Millennials proportionate representation of workforces increase, so too will their income production capacity, projected to be US$32 trillion by 2030. In the US, they will overtake other demographic groups, generating an estimated US$8.3 trillion by 2025.

- When it comes to wealth, it is estimated that in 2015, Millennials held 10 per cent (US$16.9 trillion) of the world's wealth; that is predicted to rise to US$35.3 trillion by 2020. Intergenerational wealth transfer will see this generation become the primary beneficiary of the wealth accumulated by their Baby Boomer parents.

- Millennials are the most highly-educated generation ever, with 42 per cent of 25–34 year olds in OECD countries holding a higher education degree. This has come at a significant cost in many countries through the ballooning of student debt, estimated to have reached US$1.4 trillion in the USA, £100 billion in the United Kingdom and AUD$59.7 billion in Australia.

- As Millennials spending power increases, they are predicted to overtake other demographic groups by 2028 to become the primary producer of peak profit.

- With financial security, Millennials place high importance on their personal abilities in the areas of education and flexibility. When it comes to societal factors, the job market, social networks, economic policy and family responsibilities rank highest.

Chapter Three

WORKFORCE INFLUENCE

Mind the expectation and human capital gap

> *The world is endowed with a vast wealth of human talent. The ingenuity and creativity at our collective disposal provides us with the means not only to address the great challenges of our time but also, critically, to build a future that is more inclusive and human centric.*

> **— Klaus Schwab**
> *founder and executive chairman, World Economic Forum*

In this chapter, I'll examine how Millennials see their professional life as an extension of who they are. This includes their preference to work in environments that are making a positive impact on society and how they see business playing a significant role in this pursuit.

Research reports indicate Millennials are motivated by social equity. For them, the status quo is there to be challenged. This insight would therefore help explain why organisations that have 'Massive Transformational Purposes' are more likely to be more attractive employers as they connect with Millennials emotionally. These organisations are purpose-driven, seek to play a meaningful role in society, and want to contribute to making the world a better place. That's one of the key reasons Millennials have gravitated to the start-up community and technology organisations. In developed countries, 54 per cent of Millennials have started, or plan to start, their own business, while 27 per cent are already self-employed[38]. Traditional organisations must recognise they simply can't fit Millennials into yesterday's model, because there are new models emerging that they will now have to compete against.

Millennials are predicted to represent 50 per cent of the workforce in many developed countries by 2020, and 75 per cent by 2025[39]. Yet in the last year, their confidence in business has declined, their desire for greater flexibility in the workplace and a positive work culture has increased and, most notably, Millennials are feeling unprepared for the changing nature of work. These were just some of the key findings by Deloitte[40] in their 2018 study of more than 10,000 Millennials across 36 countries.

Millennials' attitude towards corporate motives across four key indicators has reached its lowest point in the four years to 2018 (see Figure 14). Three quarters of Millennials now see businesses as focused on their own interests rather than considering the wider society. This viewpoint has increased 16 per cent since 2017. Only a minority of Millennials now believe that corporates are acting in an ethical manner and that business leaders are committed to helping improve society; a majority believe corporates have no ambition beyond wanting to make money.

Figure 14: Millennials' view of corporate motives dim (Per cent of millennials who say businesses...)

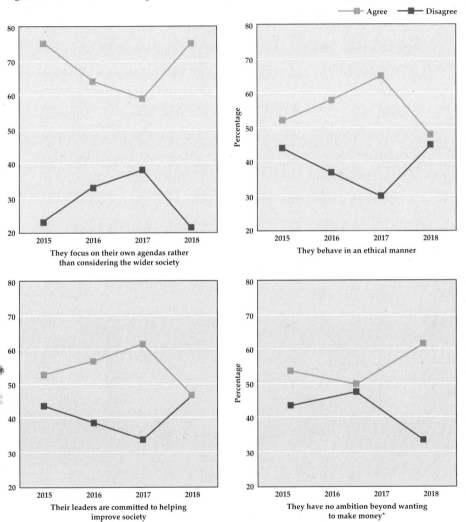

Q12. Thinking about business around the world, would you agree or disagree that, on balance, the following statements describe their current behaviour?
Base: All millennials 10,455
* "They have no ambition beyond wanting to make money" not asked in 2015

Source: Deloitte
Reproduced by permission

The study found that the underlying causes of this recent dramatic shift is down to the mismatch of priorities, with Millennials overwhelmingly feeling that business success should be measured beyond financial performance (see Figure 15). Millennials believe corporations should prioritise making a positive impact on society; create innovative ideas, products and services; develop jobs and careers; and improve people's lives, emphasising inclusion and diversity. However, they report that these priorities don't match those of their own organisations, with significant gaps in seven of the nine areas surveyed, especially regarding generating profit, driving efficiencies and producing and selling products.

Figure 15: Employers are "out of step" with millennials' priorities. Per cent of millennials who say...

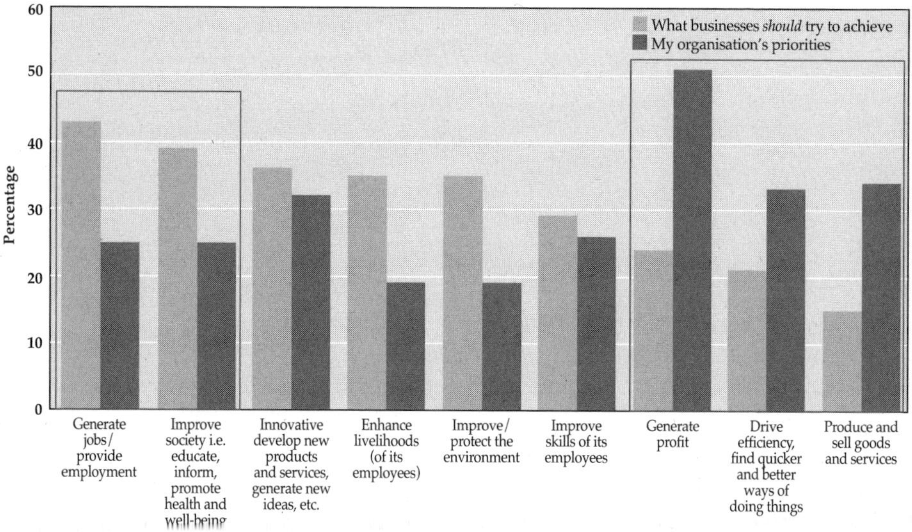

Q11a. Which of the following words and phrases match your own belief as to what business should try to achieve? Select up to three.
Base: All millennials 10,455

Source: Deloitte
Reproduced by permission

When it comes to the relationship between accountability and influence in the workplace, the 2017 Deloitte research[41] found a correlation between the two (see Figure 16). Millennials believe they have the greatest level of accountability and influence on client/customer satisfaction and working culture/atmosphere. Critically, they believe they have least influence and accountability on charitable initiatives/partnership programs and the strategic direction of the organisation. This may explain why Millennials gravitate towards the start-up ecosystem and entrepreneurship as the most important factors to empowerment.

Their perceived inability to influence the recruitment of new people and promotions reveal a broader issue of diversity. When it comes to gender, race or sexuality, we need to recognize this is the most diverse generation ever, and the vast inequalities in the workplace today will influence the choices they make on employment. I'll cover this important topic in more detail in Chapter Six.

Today's news on automation tends to focus negatively on its impact on job redundancies. Technology developments such as robotics or Artificial Intelligence are the examples usually cited. Despite this, the technologically-proficient Millennials see a different picture. Research reveals that Millennials recognize the potential economic and productivity benefits automation brings, as well as opportunities for value-added creative activities or learning new skills, with less than 9–14 per cent reporting a negative sentiment. The general concerns reported on the impact automation will have on jobs is also shared by Millennials

Figure 16: Level of accountability and influence

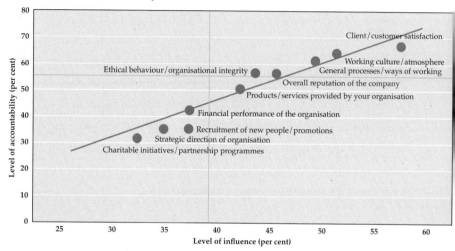

Q21. To what extent do you feel you have an influence on the following activities/issues?
Q24. How much accountability do you take for the following? By accountability we mean the level of personal responsibility you feel for ensuring they happen to the highest possible standard.

Source: Deloitte
Reproduced by permission

(36 per cent), with a majority (51 per cent) reporting a belief in the need to retrain (see Figure 17).

Millennials are well aware of the impact that the Fourth Industrial Revolution will have in the workplace. In the 2018 Millennial Survey, Deloitte found that almost four in ten Millennials reported that their organisations were making extensive use of advanced automation, advanced connectivity, Artificial Intelligence or robotics to perform mechanical tasks or analysis previously performed by people. Importantly, the study found that the majority believe the Fourth Industrial Revolution will augment their jobs, giving them more time to focus on creative, value-added work.

Figure 17: Automation sentiment (per cent)

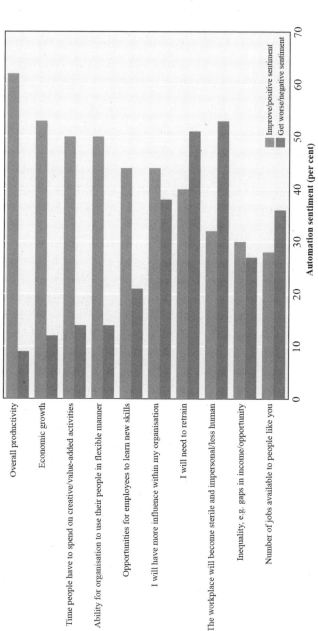

Automation sentiment (per cent)

Improve/positive sentiment
Get worse/negative sentiment

Overall productivity
Economic growth
Time people have to spend on creative/value-added activities
Ability for organisation to use their people in flexible manner
Opportunities for employees to learn new skills
I will have more influence within my organisation
I will need to retrain
The workplace will become sterile and impersonal/less human
Inequality, e.g. gaps in income/opportunity
Number of jobs available to people like you

Q32. Thinking about the future of the workplace (not just your organization but in general) do you think automation/robotics/artificial intelligence will have on the following?
Q33. What might be the impact of increasing automation/robotics/artificial intelligence in the workplace? Do you think the following will or will not apply to you?

1. According to OECD, a large share of jobs have low risk of complete automation, but an important share (between 50 and 70 per cent) of automatable task. These jobs will not be substituted entirely, but a large share of tasks may, radically transforming how these jobs are carried out. These jobs will be significantly retooled and workers will need to adapt. For more information see OECD (2016), Automations and Independent Work in a Digital Economy
http://www.oecd/employment/Automation-and-independent-work-in-a-digital-economy-2016.pdf

Whilst awareness of the Fourth Industrial Revolution and the positive sentiment on its impact in the workplace is encouraging amongst Millennials, many feel they are unprepared for the challenges it will bring. Deloitte found that only 36 per cent of Millennials believe they are fully prepared and have the skills and knowledge they need. Interestingly, Deloitte found that Millennials working in organisations that have adopted more flexible working practices (47 per cent) or have diverse senior management teams (45 per cent) have higher levels of confidence over the Fourth Industrial Revolution, as do those intending to remain longest with their employers (42 per cent). These findings support the idea that business leaders who take a holistic approach to running their organisations are better able to retain and motivate Millennial employees.

Human capital and its ongoing development transcends organisational boundaries and feeds into the prosperity of nations. According to a global study by the World Economic Forum[42], how nations develop their human capital can be a more important determinant of their long-term success than virtually any other factor. (Human capital is defined as the knowledge and skills people possess and regenerate over time, which enable them to create value in the global economic system.) As we discussed in Chapter One, with ageing populations growing faster than younger generations, human capital will become of even greater value.

This study includes The Global Human Capital Index, which ranks 130 countries on how well they are developing human capital on a scale from 0 (worst) to 100 (best). The index includes four thematic dimensions: capacity, deployment, development and know-how; and five distinct age groups or generations: 0–14 years, 15–24 years, 25–54 years, 55–64 years, and 65 years and over. What they found is fascinating:

- On average, the world has developed only 62 per cent of its human capital as measured by this index—highlighting that on average, 38 per cent of talent is underutilised. So, in a climate where we know what shortages we may be facing, this offers a significant opportunity to the supply of skills.
- There were only 25 nations that have developed 70 per cent of their people's human capital or more; 50 countries scored between 60 per cent and 70 per cent; 41 countries scored between 50 per cent and 60 per cent; and 14 countries were below 50 per cent, indicating those nations are currently leveraging less than half of their human capital.
- The top 10 countries in the Index were Norway, Finland, Switzerland, United States, Demark, Germany, New Zealand, Sweden, Slovenia and Austria.
- These leading countries generally have a longstanding commitment to their people's educational attainment and have deployed a broad share of their workforce in skill-intensive occupations. They are also today's high-income economies, indicating a virtuous cycle.
- When comparing regions, human capital development is highest in North America and Western Europe, and smallest in South Asia and Sub-Saharan Africa (see Figure 18).

Figure 18: Gap in human capital development by region 2017 (per cent)

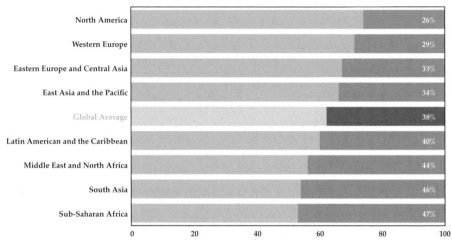

Source: Global Human Capital Index 2017; World Economic Form, Switzerland 2017

Attracting, retaining and developing human capital is paramount to the future performance of any nation or organisation, public or private. Evolving the workplace environment, policies and culture for continuous learning and adapting to technological advancements is even more critical, as it needs to keep up with a world changing faster than we've ever known.

This process will be further complicated as Millennials increase their proportionate mix in an organisation's workforce, and also in the balance between human capital investment and technology investment. The Korn Ferry Institute[43] commissioned a global economic analysis to consider this question by interviewing 800 leaders of multi-million dollar global organisations about their views on where growth and value would be generated in the future. They found that:

- 63 per cent saw that in five year's time, technology will be their firm's greatest source of competitive advantage
- 67 per cent believe that technology will create greater value in the future than people
- 44 per cent think that robotics, automation, and Artificial Intelligence will make people 'largely irrelevant' in the future of work; and
- when they ranked the top five assets for their organisation in the next five years, they listed technology, R&D, product and service, brand, and real estate; human capital didn't make the list.

Ironically enough, human capital is fundamental to the top five assets ranked by business leaders, yet it is in the shadows. We need to reprioritise our thinking and put people ahead of technology, R&D, products and services, brand and real estate, and rebalance strategies on how to better utilise human capital.

Trust the young people; trust this generation's innovation. They're making things, changing innovation every day.

— Jack Ma
founder and executive chairman, Alibaba Group

Chapter summary

- In developed countries, 54 per cent of Millennials started, or plan to start, their own business, while 27 per cent are already self-employed. Traditional organisations must recognize they simply can't fit them into yesterday's model, because there are new models emerging that they will now compete for skills with.

- Millennials believe they have the greatest accountability for client and customer satisfaction and culture, yet they report having the least influence on an organisation's strategic direction.

- This perception, on the inability to influence an organisation's strategic direction, may partly explain why they see the start-up ecosystem and entrepreneurship as the most important route to empowerment.

- Millennials recognize the opportunities of automation in improving productivity, economic growth, creation/value-added activities, flexibility, learning new skills and influence.

- How nations and organisations develop their human capital can be a more important determinant of their long-term success than virtually any other factor. Yet today, on average the world has developed only 62 per cent of its human capital, highlighting that on average, 38 per cent of their talent is underutilised.

- Despite this, global business leaders don't rank human capital in their top five assets in the next five years.

- Millennials' confidence in business has declined and their desire for greater flexibility in the workplace and a positive work culture has increased, while they feel unprepared for the changing nature of work.

- Millennials view of corporate behaviour has reached its lowest point in four years. Three quarters of Millennials see business around the world focusing on their own agendas rather than considering the wider society.

Chapter Four

TECHNOLOGICAL, MEDIA AND INNOVATION INFLUENCE

The sixth sense

> *For Millennials, technology is a sixth sense. It's a way of knowing the world. There is no real cognitive processing like there is for other generations who learn it later in life.*

— Andrea Hershatter
Senior Associate Dean, Emory University

The first time I realised that my kids (and indeed all others) had this 'sixth sense' was when we were driving through the country on route to visit my family, who lived on a farm in a remote part of Australia. It was a beautiful autumn day, two hours into a six-hour drive; the sun was shining, with picture-perfect rolling fields of green and sheep grazing. From nowhere, one of those green fields caught my attention. That field had 12 massive satellite dishes pointed upward to the sky and strategically placed around that field—this was the strangest thing I had ever seen and so out of character with the landscape. There was no signage on the road or in the field to indicate what the installation was or its purpose. Immediately I thought it must be a scientific or agricultural installation from one of Australia's research institutions—either that, or the farmer who owned the property had an obsession with some sport not broadcast through local television networks.

Given how unusual this was in a rural setting, I brought the sighting to my kids' attention, who at the time naturally had their heads at 45 degrees with eyes locked onto entertainment emitting from their smartphones screens, delivering audio at full volume through their earpieces into their little ears. Expecting questions of physics or perhaps astronomy, I braced myself for the tough questions that these eager, inquisitive young minds would pose. Raising their heads from their smartphone screens to observe this communication installation, in unison, and with excitement in their eyes they asked: 'Do you think we could get free Wi-Fi from it, Daddy?' I realised in that moment, that for this generation, the sight of communication infrastructure did not correlate to physics or astronomy; but in fact what I was observing was a generational biological phenomenon. To them, being connected is as natural as breathing, and being disconnected was an unnatural state. I was then left with three very disappointed (and still unconnected) kids to contend with for the next four hours, but with the knowledge that our youth have grown up in a *mobile- and media-first world.*

Technology has connected, informed, empowered and entertained the Millennial generation. As discussed earlier, 86 per cent of the Millennial population live in emerging markets. To many, wireless technology is their first and only form of connectivity and a critical link to digital inclusion. For example, of the 2.5 billion people in lower and middle-income countries that don't have bank accounts, one billion have access to a mobile phone.

The Bill and Melinda Gates 2014 Annual Review predicted as one of the top five bets that by 2030 two billion people will be storing money and making payments on mobile devices (referring to the unbanked and under-banking communities[44]). Mobile technology today supports 277 live mobile money services in 92 countries—these will be a critical link to financial inclusion for 400 million users in emerging markets that today are unbanked. So mobile technology has not only been fundamental to digital inclusion, but also financial inclusion.

Mobile internet penetration is predicted to increase from 48 per cent in 2016 to 60 per cent by 2020 globally, adding approximately one billion more unique mobile subscribers and 1.9 billion smartphones, raising the smartphone penetration to 5.7 billion globally[45]. The smartphone has also become the primary device for our social connections, with an estimated three billion active mobile social users[46]. Let's just pause and think about that.

Imagine for a moment what impact connecting one billion more people will do for digital, economic and social inclusion. What entrepreneurship and innovation will this bring to the world? In 2016, the United Nations declared the internet a 'human right'[47]. Article 19 of the Universal Declaration of Human Rights (UDHR) states: 'Everyone has the right to freedom of opinion and expression; this right includes freedom to hold opinions without interference and to seek, receive and impart information and ideas through any media and regardless of frontiers.' Section 32 of Article 19 includes: 'The promotion, protection and enjoyment of human rights on the Internet.'

Millennials have not only grown up with wireless technology, they will most likely drive the demand for future devices, networks, services and media due to their technological proficiency and ever-increasing expectation levels. It is what social researcher Mark McCrindle refers to as 'expectation inflation'[48].

If we consider for a moment the time that it took key technologies to be adopted, the smartphone has broken all records (see Figure 19). It took just six years to achieve 70 per cent adoption in the US population, reflecting the exponential effect of this technology; and Millennials are widely reported as being more smartphone penetrated than other demographic group in many countries.

In a very short time, an economy valued in trillions has emerged. Beyond devices, services and network subscriptions, in just 10 years an app economy has reached an estimated value of US$1.3 trillion in 2016, driven by 3.4 billion users spending more than 1.6 trillion hours using apps; this equates to an average US$379 per person from mobile apps, in-app advertising and mobile commerce[49]. The exponential growth of this economy is projected to rise five-fold to US$6.3 trillion by 2021, as device-based growth virtually doubles to 6.3 billion users in 2021, averaging US$1,008 per person.

Figure 19: Years taken for technology to be adopted by per cent of US population

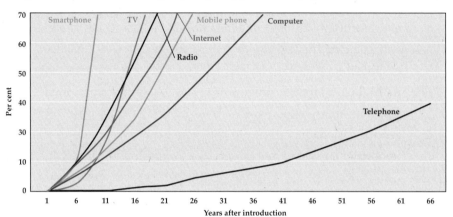

Note: Market penetration is a percent of US households (telephone, electricity, radio, TV, internet) or percent of US consumers (smartphone, tablet)

Source: BI Intelligence
Reproduced by permission

We have, indeed, become a 'planet of the apps'. Since 2015, app downloads increased 60 per cent to 175 billion, and consumer spending increased 105 per cent to US$86 billion. The average smartphone user, particularly in those countries that have heavy concentrations of Millennials, such as India, China, Brazil, Indonesia, South Korea, United States, Germany, France, United Kingdom, Japan and Mexico, now has an average of 80 apps on their device, 40 of which are used monthly. There has not been any technology in history that has had such a profound impact on our behaviour in such a short time as mobile applications.

Understanding our rapidly changing behaviour and engagement with this technology is therefore paramount for most organisations, as is the need to adapt our traditional models of understanding behaviour and segmentation. The GSMA developed a Global Mobile Engagement Index (GMEI),[50] which is a useful tool to help understand what's behind our mobile engagement. The GMEI is based on the mobile usage patterns of more than 50,000 survey respondents across 50 countries. The index helps interpret engagement levels among smartphone and non-smartphone owners across an array of use cases and services. The higher the score, the more likely consumers are to frequently engage in mobile services. Supporting the index, the GSMA developed a consumer segmentation methodology that produced four segments:

- **Talkers** use mobile phones almost exclusively to make a voice call or send an SMS
- **Networkers** mostly use phones to communicate, socialise, browse the internet and for apps, and occasionally for entertainment
- **Pragmatists** show high usage across most areas, but are still experimenting with lifestyle, digital commerce and financial services
- **Aficionados** show the highest engagement across all use case categories.

They found that Millennials are the most engaged globally, with more than half of aficionados globally.

So as Millennials' engagement through devices increases, so will their economic engagement (and their experience expectations). These expectations will play an important role in shaping mobile services, particularly on fifth generation (5G) networks. Video consumption trends demonstrate the shift of video into mobile devices for Millennials.

According to a study of 14,000 smartphone users across 14 countries by Ericsson,[51] 50 per cent of Millennials stream on-demand video, 28 per cent of which is for one-to-three hours per day, six times more than those aged 45 or over. They place higher importance on the personalisation of content than older demographic groups. This consumption has led this demographic to also become more critical and less tolerant of network performance than older groups, with less than half of Millennial smartphone users satisfied with their mobile broadband quality. Not only do they have very high expectations of speed, coverage and reliability from 5G, but also content responsiveness, improved battery life of their devices and security of their personal information (see Figure 20).

Figure 20: Millennials 5G expectation

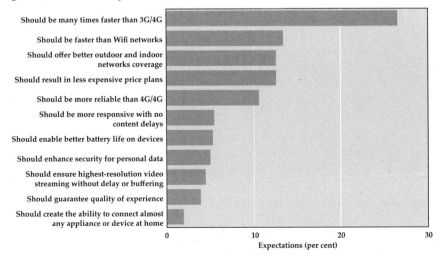

Source: Ericsson ComsumerLab Analytical Platform (June 2017)
Reproduced by permission

The road to 5G networks is continuously evolving. Hype on the possibilities of these networks is reaching fever pitch, with billions of objects, devices, sensors and other technologies yet to be imagined. One thing is for sure: if experience expectations are being challenged on 4G networks, they will be even more so with 5G, and expectations of zero latency being promoted by mobile operators will be put to the test.

Speed-to-content is the new king. Early in our digital revolution content became king, but as we move into the Fourth Industrial Revolution, it's the speed of access to that content that has become the new king. Latency has become an important indicator of expectation for Millennials experiencing mobile, on-demand video services. A neuroscience study by Ericsson and Vodafone[52] to understand the impact of varying network performance on smartphone users found a direct correlation between consumers' subconscious (emotional responses) and physical reactions to time-to-content on mobile apps (see Figure 21). The study revealed some interesting insights:

- Heart rate rises by 44 per cent for Millennials who experience delays of just two seconds while uploading their selfie, referred to as 'selfie stress'.
- With the AutoPlay feature, any video loading delays on Facebook were found to be more stressful than delays on YouTube.
- Millennial and streaming natives were found to be less tolerant to delays in loading online videos, with 35 per cent more stressed with mobile delays than non-Millennials.

Figure 21: Stress caused by time-to-content video delays among age groups 18-24, 25-34, 35+

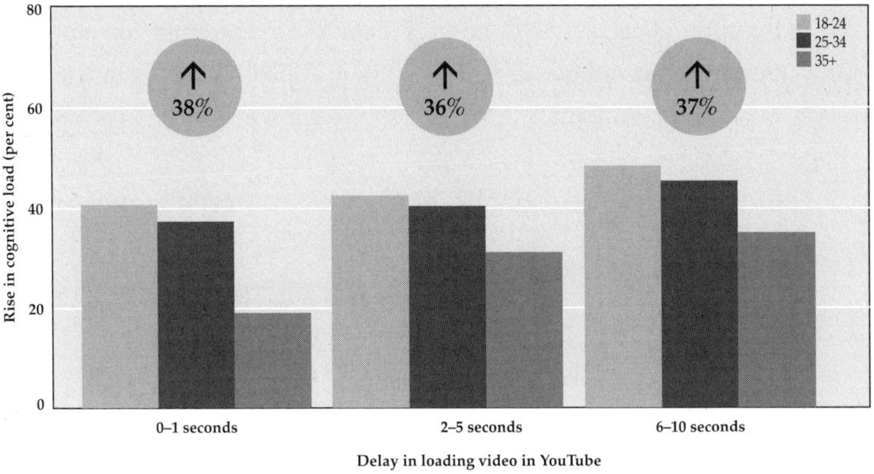

Source: Ericsson ComsumerLab in a blink of an eye (June 2016)

- Millennials were most stressed at six seconds or more of video delays, and after eight seconds they'd completely lost interest in watching the video.

Millennials gave rise to the use of both social media and camera technology in smartphones that contributed the word 'selfie' to our vocabulary. Oxford Dictionaries named it word of the year in 2013 after it was first used by an Australian describing a photograph taken while intoxicated at a 21st birthday party. What the Ericsson and Vodafone study has now identified is that delays in uploading selfies leads to stress. For example, a one-second delay led to a significant rise in cognitive demand, with stress levels rising for 47 per cent of participants, and with a two-second delay 47 per cent of participants lost interest in the task. After eight seconds, most participants gave up trying to upload their selfie. The key point here is that the expectation inflation effect needs to be very carefully considered for any organisation in how they design their apps or services in the experience economy.

Millennials are increasingly using live video streaming apps to share experiences, information and to interact with their friends and communities, enabled by streaming apps such as Facebook and Twitter. Millennials remain the dominant demographic using major social media platforms. For example, as of January 2018, they represented the largest demographic using Facebook (57 per cent of total users) and Instagram (60 per cent of total users)[53].

However, when it comes to communication with their closest friends, social media ranks last for most Millennial sub ages, with texting (38.8 per cent) first for all ages, speaking in person 23.5 per cent for all ages, other than the 22–30 year age group, where it ranks marginally third behind social media (see Figure 22).

We should recognise the importance of both person-to-person communication and omni-channel communication—it isn't an either/or option. The difference between Millennials and other generations is that they have become accustomed to an omni-digital world. This means that in the past, we may have visited a physical bank branch to discuss something with a skilled person, but Millennials are happy to have that interaction using FaceTime on multiple digital devices.

Figure 22: How do you communciate the most frequently with your closest friends? (N=20432)

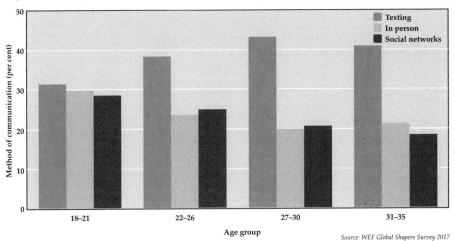

Source: WEF Global Shapers Survey 2017

As high-speed connectivity, smartphones and cloud computing become ubiquitous, they are giving rise to next-generation technologies. One of those is Artificial Intelligence. The development of this exponential technology is being led by major global technology companies such as IBM and Microsoft and internet companies such as Apple, Google, Amazon and Facebook. Natural language processing allows technology to understand humans, transforming the user interface and how we interact with devices.

The technologically-proficient Millennials understand the significance of this technological development and hence believe that the next big technology trends will come from AI (28 per cent), biotechnology (11.5 per cent), robotics (9.3 per cent) and driverless cars (7.1 per cent) (see Figure 23). These are just some of the critical next-generation technologies associated with the

Figure 23: According to you, what is the next big technology trend? (N=21115)

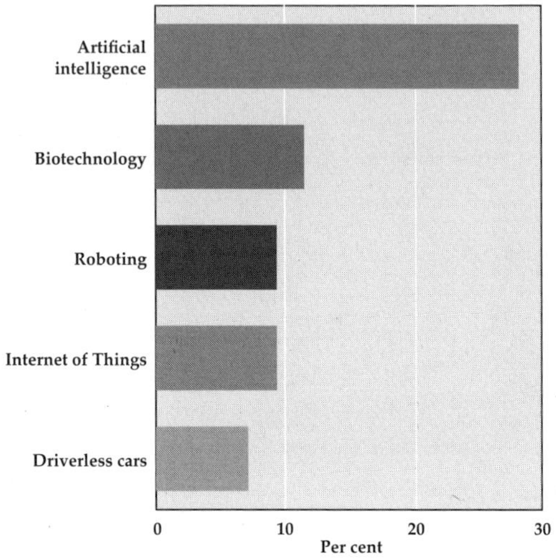

Source: WEF Global Shapers Survey 2017

Fourth Industrial Revolution that I'll cover in more detail in Chapter 10.

When it comes to assessing how these technologies would benefit industries, Millennials clearly prioritise education, healthcare, manufacturing and energy (see Figure 24). Of interest is that they see financial services last among these industries, yet it's one of the early adopting industries of Artificial Intelligence technologies. However, while recognising the potential benefit of these technologies on industries, we still have a significant transformative road ahead, with many industries still struggling to capitalise on all the benefits from the technologies associated with the Third Industrial Revolution. (In Chapter Eight, we'll explore what's holding back industries.)

**Figure 24: In your country, which sector do you think would benefit
the most from the adoption of the latest technologies (N=21078)**

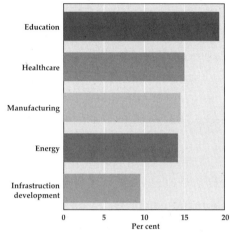

Percentage of unique votes. Respondents were allowed to select up to three answer choices.
Next choice were *Agriculture* (7.4%), *Government* (6.8%), *Finance* (5.2%)

Source: WEF Global Shapers Survey 2017

Figure 25: In your opinion, technology is... (N=2105-9)

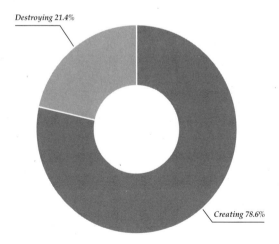

Source: WEF Global Shapers Survey 2017

Contrary to popular commentary about the fears associated with the loss of jobs from new technologies such as AI, an overwhelming number of Millennials think that technology creates jobs (78.6 per cent) as opposed to destroying jobs (21.4 per cent) (see Figure 25). This is unsurprising given the technological proficiency of this generation, but does emphasise the optimism they have for technology's role in business and the workplace.

For many years, science fiction has filled our imaginations with the possibilities of technologies—many of which have become a reality—while many remain as an undeveloped sixth sense, such as the augmentation of human life with new technology. I'll close this chapter by posing a question: how willing (and ready) would you be to embrace some of those ideas? Well, when faced with the possibility of having an implant under their skin or in their brain to increase their capabilities, 44.3 per cent of Millennials rejected the idea. Of interest, however, is that 30 per cent of males were willing to have the implant, versus 17.3 per cent of females—have we identified an early adopter segment?

The factory of the future will have only two employees—a man, and a dog. The man will be there to feed the dog. The dog will be there to keep the man from touching the equipment.

— **Warren G. Bennis**
scholar, organisational consultant, author

Chapter summary

- Millennials have grown up in a mobile media first world, which has inflated their expectations of the services consumed through their smartphones.

- Understanding our rapidly changing behaviour and engagement with mobile technology is paramount for most organisations, as is the need to adapt our traditional models of understanding behaviour and segmentation.

- Next-generation 5G networks will be a critical enabler for many of the emerging technologies in the Fourth Industrial Revolution.

- Avoid creating 'selfie stress'—time-to-content has now become a major experience expectation.

- While social media is the primary media consumed by Millennials, texting and face-to-face communications are preferred and the most frequently used method of communicating with friends. We now need to consider interactions in an omni-digital sense as this generation gave rise to 'face-time'.

- Millennials believe that the next big technology trends will be in Artificial Intelligence, biotechnology, robotics and driverless cars.

- They believe these technologies will benefit the education, healthcare, manufacturing, energy and infrastructure development industries the most.

- Overwhelmingly, Millennials see technology as creating jobs, not destroying them.

Chapter Five

INTERCONNECTED TRUST

The digital economy's renewable energy

> *The implications of the global trust*
> *crisis are deep and wide-ranging.*

— Richard Edelman
president and CEO Edelman

Trust is the genesis of our beliefs as they relate to spirituality, society, culture, economies and technologies. That is why this chapter is the bridge between Section 1 of this book, Youthquake, and Section 2 of this book, the Fourth Industrial Revolution. The conditions upon which we trust people, ideas and platforms—the 'trust trinity'—have profoundly shifted away from a hierarchical-based, vertical model concentrated in the hands of institutions in which we have lost faith, in favour of a democratised, horizontal model that distributes trust among communities at a global scale, real-time speed. It is the 'renewable energy' of our digital society, culture and economies, and the technologies that are intertwined in the way we live, work and play.

In this chapter, I've draw upon the cutting-edge thought leadership of Rachel Botsman. In *Who Can You Trust?*[54], Botsman's central argument is that 'institutional trust, taken on faith, kept in the hands of a few and operating behind closed doors, wasn't designed for the digital age'. It lacks transparency, creates transactional friction, and is unfit for the gig economy, being misaligned with our platform dependency and with the personalisation that now empowers us through our devices. She proposes that we need to shift to a more contemporary model. Her point is that despite the failings of the existing trust model, it should not be destroyed, but rather adapted and changed to fit with our digital society. The time for this adaption is now, as it is the critical enabler to the next stage of our digital evolution.

In 2017, trust in four key institutions—business, government, NGOs and media—has declined and hit a global crisis point. The 2017 Edelman Trust Barometer[55] across 28 countries found that the majority of the 33,000-plus respondents (53 per cent) don't believe the system is working for them, is unfair, and offers little hope for the future[56]. Only 15 per cent believe it is working, with the rest uncertain. Without trust, belief in the system fails. People's societal and economic concerns, globalisation, the pace of innovation and eroding social values are creating fears across the world.

Trust declined in media by 43 per cent to all-time lows in 17 countries, while trust in government fell by 41 per cent in 14 countries, becoming the least trusted in half of the 28 countries in the study. Business is heavily distrusted (52 per cent) with a fall in 18 countries, yet, of the four institutional types, 75 per cent of respondents reported business to be the only one that can make a difference (through profit increase, improved economic conditions, social conditions). Credibility of CEOs fell 12 per cent globally to an all-time low of 37 per cent in every country studied, marking this moment in time as an inflection point upon which renewal requires new thinking and leadership.

When it comes to the impact that this erosion of trust has had on our digital lives, all the signposts point in the same direction: crisis. Whether it is cyber-attacks or economic loss, all the indicators lead us to the same conclusion. That is, as the Edelman study shows, our digital lives are also at the same inflection point. Let us examine one of the most important indicators of this: data breaches.

According to Gemalto, a global digital security solutions provider, its Breach Level Index indicates that in the first half of 2017, there were more than two billion records data breaches reported around the world (see Figure 26)[57]—a staggering 164 per cent increase on the previous six months. The Index is not a complete picture, as there were more than 500 data breaches that had an unknown or unreported number of compromised records. Mandatory data breach notification regulations, such as the General Data Protection Regulation (GDPR) in Europe and Australia's Privacy Act, will improve reporting of these events as they become enforceable in 2018. Identity theft accounted for a staggering three quarters of data breaches—an increase of 49 per cent compared to the previous six months. A notable identity theft occurred in Britain's National Health

Service, which reported a loss of 26 million records. Another was the Deep Root Analytics, contracted by the United States' Republican National Committee, which reported a data breach involving 198 million records.

Financial access was the next most common attack, accounting for 13 per cent of the total reported breaches. The number of records stolen increased 17 per cent from the previous six months. At an industry level, the healthcare sector reported the highest number of breaches, representing 25 per cent of the total. Approximately 31 million records were stolen, up 423 per cent from the previous six months. While healthcare, financial services and education were the most impacted industries, the index highlights that all industries, including government, are increasingly exposed to data breaches. At a regional level, North America experienced the highest number of breaches, representing 88 per cent of the worldwide total. This was a 23 per cent increase on the previous year.

The impact of these breaches on people across all aspects of their lives, and their digital lives, serves to further erode the trust in the institutions that are the custodians of their personal information.

So, if we ask who Millennials believe should play the greatest role in making the world a better place, we get a very interesting answer. Millennials believe individuals have the greatest role to play (see Figure 27). This empowered generation is not relying on institutions to guide change, but rather individuals.

Figure 26: Reported data breaches (1st half 2017)

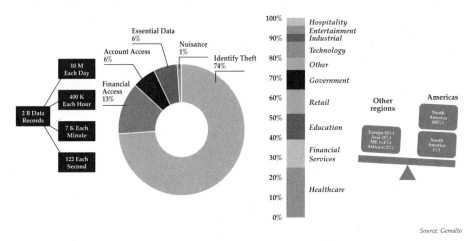

Source: Gemalto

Figure 27: Who has the greatest role to play in making the world a better place? (N=24272)

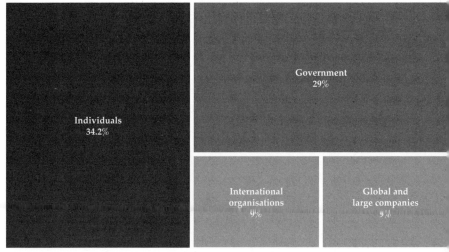

Source: WEF Global Shapers Survey 2017

The broader findings in the Edelman Trust Barometer study are correlated at a generational level by Millennials. As a highly-educated generation, Millennials trust academics/school institutions the most on values of fairness and honesty. In addition to their parents, education was the next most powerful influence on them. They also believe that their employers are fair and honest, with one in two reporting so. At the opposite end of the spectrum are national government organisations who are the least trusted, reflecting their scepticism around political parties and also news media and religious institutions, which attracted worldwide attention for their inadequate treatment of child abuse (see Figure 28).

Interestingly, banks are ranked third-last at 28.2 per cent in overall institutional trust for fairness and honesty. However, when considering who Millennials trust most to hold and

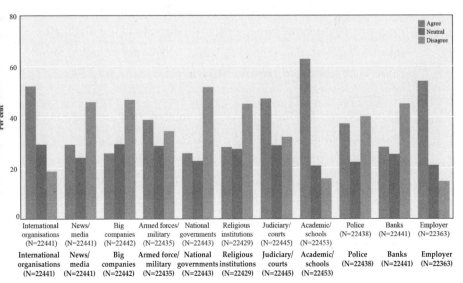

Source: WEF Global Shapers Survey 2017

maintain the privacy and security of personal information, we get a completely different picture.

In a separate study of 6,000-plus Millennials across 10 countries, it was unanimous: financial services, including banks and card schemes, ranked number one by 43 per cent, and highest in India and the United States with 60 per cent-plus (see Figure 29). So why don't Millennials believe banks to be fair and honest, yet trust them with sensitive personal information? It points to the fact that trust has a number of dimensions. It is highly contextual and fragmented. Importantly, this is why the hierarchical trust model no longer serves our needs in a digital world. We need models that are more transparent and collaborative.

A significant opportunity exists for banks to leverage the personal information entrusted to them by Millennials to improve their reputation as the 'safest hands'. As our digital experiences and footprint exponentially increases, so do the risks of identity theft, fraud and cybercrime. However, banks will require collaboration from other ecosystem providers to win trust.

When it comes to our personal information, new or emerging technology companies, comparison websites and digital-only banks were reported as the least trusted by Millennials (25 per cent) at a global average and by all 10 countries. The gap between banks and these disruptive players (18 per cent) provides banks with a significant margin to leverage from. However, trust is perishable and with increasing cyber-attacks and identity theft, this window will likely be challenged over time.

Figure 29: Please indicate the extent to which you trust the following to hold and maintain the privacy and security of your personal information

% Highly likely to trust organisation (8+/10)
Milllennials

	Australia	Canada	China	France	Hong-Kong	India	Mexico	Singapore	UK	US	Global average
Banks	34%	42%	53%	24%	26%	63%	55%	34%	37%	60%	43%
Card schemes/brands	27%	31%	44%	23%	18%	60%	56%	30%	35%	54%	38%
Government agencies	27%	28%	51%	17%	23%	55%	32%	33%	25%	51%	34%
Technology companies	22%	24%	38%	12%	14%	60%	52%	23%	28%	55%	33%
Telecommunications providers	22%	22%	38%	13%	12%	56%	36%	20%	22%	50%	29%
Retailers	20%	20%	35%	14%	13%	48%	44%	21%	26%	48%	29%
New digital-only banks/FinTechs	18%	15%	40%	11%	11%	50%	29%	15%	18%	46%	25%
Price comparison sites	18%	14%	31%	12%	10%	46%	32%	18%	23%	47%	25%
New or emerging technology companies	18%	13%	32%	10%	9%	48%	35%	17%	17%	49%	25%
Most trusted:	Banks	Banks	Banks	Banks	Banks	Banks	Card schemes	Banks	Banks	Banks	Banks

Source: RFi Intelligence

This trust fragmentation across the values of fairness and honesty, and that of personal information in Millennials' digital lives, suggests that the old hierarchal model identified by Botsman where trust is vested in the few institutions, is unlikely to provide adequate renewal of trust for a digital world.

Let us now consider what sources do Millennials trust and rely upon when it comes to online content. We know Millennials care about what they read, where it's sourced and that it's credible and trustworthy. Less than one-in-three Millennials trust news/media on fairness and honesty (as we saw in Figure 29), well behind seven other organisational types. At a content level, the reputation of the content originator is the primary factor in what makes content trustworthy online (see Figure 30).

Figure 30: What makes content trustworthy on the internet? (N=20908)

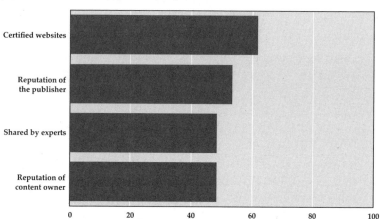

Percentage of unique votes. Respondents were allowed to choose up to three choices.

Source: WEF Global Shapers Survey 2017

Despite their pervasive use of social media, over 77 per cent of Millennials do not rely on it as a source of trusted news (see Figure 31). This is another important myth that needs busting.

As we saw in Chapter Four, Millennials represent about 57 per cent of Facebook uses. In 2016, Facebook made changes to its personal news-feed algorithm that promotes content posted by friends above content by traditional media outlets. This fundamentally changes the diversity of news and authors from certified websites, reputable publishers and experts rated by Millennials for making internet content trustworthy. The impulse for this change cannot be explained in customer-centric logic—after all, the prime motivation of users of Facebook is for social networking, not accessing media. However, it may be explained commercially, given that 41.4 per cent of traffic to media sites is directed from Facebook. While Facebook claims it is a neutral technology platform that facilitates connection between people and content, including reputable news, it is clear that the reputation of publishers and experts influences Millennials most when considering what makes content trustworthy. The fact that news/media ranked the third least trusted on fairness and honesty (see Figure 28) highlights the reputational challenges these organisations face in engaging with Millennials.

Figure 31: I trust the news I see on social media (N=20441)

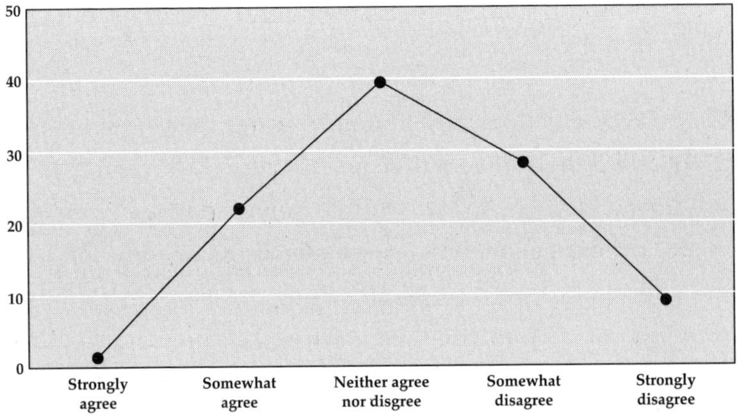

Source: WEF Global Shapers 2017

Reputation

Reputation is everything to Millennials when it comes to trusting online content. Reputation is central to gauging the loyalty of an organisation's customer relationships. Net promoter score (NPS) is a management tool that is used widely to measure customer experience and predict growth. It is reportedly used by more than two-thirds of Fortune 1000 companies[58]. Reputation is typically surveyed by asking the question: 'On a scale of 0 to 10, how likely are you to recommend this company's product or service to a friend or a colleague.'

So, in the past, garnering your trust to recommend became the NPS's logic to support the data of its predictive methodology. However, technology platforms have extended our circle of trust exponentially and globally to reach much broader networks, beyond friends and family, to now include strangers or 'likes'. These are people we don't know, yet we rely on their independent reviews or ratings to make decisions. We now have a lot more 'noise' to filter.

We make these decisions routinely, using reviews on travel destinations, accommodation on Airbnb, Uber rides, news, goods and services. While we may know that some reviews might be exaggerated or even gamed, they form part of the information we seek to make our decisions. What other people think about a product, service, organisation or person is based on past experiences that have accumulated over time or the reputation of the individual giving the review, which forms a measure of trustworthiness. These platforms make both sides of the transaction accountable, but not infallible. Reputation, therefore, is what Botsman describes as 'trust's closet sibling'.

But technology and machines also require trust and reputation, particularly in light of the tsunami of sensors, objects, devices, robotic and autonomous vehicles now in development and use. How would you feel skiing down a slope when you're overtaken by a robot on skis? What if they pushed in to the lift queue? What are the protocols? How do you address the intrusive machine?

How would you feel about driverless cars and drones transporting you and other passengers to work and back? What do you say to the drone that delivers your pizza order to your front door, when the order is missing the garlic bread? What will the neighbours think when they see you debating the order with the drone? How would you feel about swallowing a capsule containing nanotechnology for a medical treatment?

While these scenarios may not be possible today, working through the ethical, moral and other issues will require us to consider every aspect of trust, as well as the potential for unintended consequences. How we establish, maintain and re-establish trust with technology when it fails is not something new to us. I'm sure we've all experienced our computers, cars, appliances, smartphones, ATMs or other equipment malfunctioning at some stage.

As citizens, we have relied on government policy and the certification authorities, communities, industries, and markets to reflect the moral and social values of society. We have depended upon those entities for the establishment, supervision and management of trust, and we will be asking even more of them in a world that is changing exponentially.

Our relationship with technology is asynchronous. Our trust in technology is primarily centred on its functionality and the reputation of the manufacturer.

But this is now changing. Our relationship with emerging technologies is becoming synchronous; our trust is shifting from trusting the technology and the reputation of the manufacturer to perform a task, to one that makes decisions and carries them out. These are decisions that put our lives in the hands of a software program that thinks and learns. It becomes artificially intelligent.

How do we trust technology?

This is the question many of us are asking today, with technologies such as Artificial Intelligence permeating many aspects of our lives. For example, we ask Chatbots daily for information or to book taxis. Medical practitioners are using this technology to improve patient healthcare. After all, without trust, we simply won't use it right.

Botsman's research suggests that part of the answer can be explained with anthropomorphism—where the technology has human-like tendencies and qualities, emotions and appearances. Studies have identified that self-driving vehicles that include anthropomorphic features via voice interactivity increased trial participants' trust in the driverless vehicle. Early speech recognition systems and the first generation of interactive technologies blurred the boundaries between human and non-human. Researchers believe that we have a tendency to anthropomorphise technology because we are more likely to trust things that look and sound like us.

How do Millennials feel about trusting a robot to make decisions?

This generation may be technologically proficient and empowered and lack trust in major institutions, yet half of them don't trust robots to make decisions on their behalf, but one in four does (see Figure 32).

Figure 32: I would trust decisions made by a robot on my behalf (N=20962)

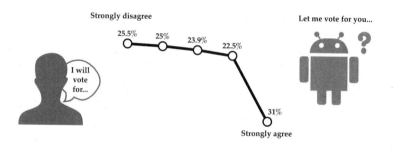

Source: WEF Global Shapers Survey 2017

Distributed trust

Distributed trust is defined as trust that flows laterally between individuals, enabled by networks, platforms and systems[59]. Distributed trust is underpinned by the principle of 'decentralisation', where authority is transferred to uses away from central authorities such as governments, institutions, banks or businesses. It disperses functions, powers, people or things away from requiring an intermediary to confirm trust, where the network of computers confirms trust through a shared ledger recorded on a blockchain. The record is mathematically proven and hence immutable. At a time where trust in our institutions is in crisis, blockchain technology empowers users in unimaginable ways, and is hence a key emerging technology in the Fourth Industrial Revolution. I'll cover that in more detail in Chapter 10.

As a trust technology, blockchain has features that provide real-time validation, non-repudiation, configuration verification, and transfer of risk. For example, blockchain can provide:

- Validation of transaction chains, such as Bitcoin
- Settlements for international financial payments, or share trading
- Data flows, as with smart contracts
- Chain of custody, which has important applications in the agricultural and pharmaceutical industries, where preparations can be tracked from providence to end user through supply-chain mapping

Blockchain has also been referred to as the 'internet of value', since the technology is a very significant transformative overlay on the internet that disaggregates, disintermediates and dematerialises value chains across many industries. Futurist Marc Andreessen has called it the most important technology since the development of the internet itself[60].

Let's now bring these points together To adapt trust to accommodate our digital lives, and its coverage to include additional actors operating in a decentralised and real-time way, requires extending the topology from a centralised hierarchical position into a decentralised position. I call this 'interconnected trust' (see Figure 33), where actors or assets can be commissioned to perform the trust element within the synchronicity desired by the activity.

Figure 33: Interconnected trust

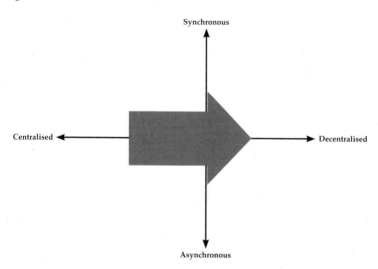

Is trust the most important enabler for all that the Fourth Industrial Revolution has to offer? Let's explore that next.

It is trust, more than money,
that makes the world go around.[61]

— Joseph Stiglitz

Chapter summary

- Trust is in crisis globally and declining across four key institutions: business, government, NGOs and media.

- Reported data breaches are primarily targeting our identity, healthcare and financial accounts. These breaches are growing at exponential rates.

- People's societal and economic concerns, globalisation, the pace of innovation and eroding social values are creating fears across the world.

- Millennials are not looking to institutions but rather to individuals to play the greatest role in making the world a better place.

- Millennials believe our educators and experts hold the greatest trust with the key values of fairness and honesty.

- Despite banks being one of the least trusted institution types at a values level, they are the most trusted when it comes to the protection of their personal information.

- Reputation is the most significant factor of the trustworthiness of content on the internet.

- Our relationship with emerging technologies is becoming synchronous, where our trust shifts from trusting the technology and the reputation of the manufacturer to perform a task, to one trusting the technology to make decisions and carry them out.

- Distributed trust is underpinned by the principle of 'decentralisation', where authority is transferred to uses away from central authorities such as governments, institutions, banks or businesses.

- In the context of trust, it disperses functions, powers, people or things away from requiring an intermediary to confirm trust, where the network of computers confirms trust through a shared ledger recorded on a blockchain.

- The conditions upon which we trust people, ideas and platforms—
  the 'trust trinity'—have profoundly shifted away from a hierarchical-
  based vertical model, concentrated in the hands of institutions that
  we've lost faith in, in favour of a democratized horizontal model that
  distributes trust among communities at global scale, in real-time
  speed, with a symmetrical impact.

- Renewing trust to accommodate the evolution of our digital lives
  requires extending the topology to an interconnected model,
  accommodating more actors operating in a decentralised model.

YOUTH QUAKE 4.0

WELCOME TO THE FOURTH INDUSTRIAL REVOLUTION

Chapter Six

BUSINESS AND THE WORKPLACE

Purpose, inclusion, diversity

> *On any given day, I analyse the binomial*
> *levels of air displacement, friction, and velocity.*
> *And compute over 10,000 calculations by cosine,*
> *square root, and lately analytic geometry. By hand.*

> **— Katherine Johnson (played by Taraji Henson),**
> *Job Title: Computer, from 2016 movie* Hidden Figures

How has labour adapted to each industrial revolution?

We begin this chapter by reviewing labour market history across the industrial revolutions and consider the impact they had on industries and work practices. We will also cover the biggest untapped business opportunity of the 21st century—gender and demographic diversity.

The wonderful 2016 movie *Hidden Figures* reminds us of just how far we have come in a relatively short period of time, but yet, from a gender diversity perspective, how far we've got to go. Katherine Johnson is an African-American mathematician known for accuracy in computerised celestial navigation. She made contributions to the US's aeronautics and space programs with the early application of computers at NASA. Katherine began work in 1953 with the National Advisory Committee for Aeronautics (NACA) (superseded by NASA in 1958), working in a pool of women performing mathematical calculations. She referred to the women in the pool as 'virtual computers who wore skirts'. Today, that time-consuming work can be done in milliseconds with an in-memory computer.

Just as in-memory computing transformed calculating by hand (and made jobs like Katherine's much easier), digital technologies are transforming the way we work today—and making our day-to-day activities more efficient.

If we consider the impact technology has had on employment over the First, Second and Third Industrial Revolutions using the United States as an example, we can see that while it has created major industry shifts it has also created significant levels of new employment (see Figure 34).

The First Industrial Revolution (1700–1870) saw a period of mechanisation of the agricultural, manufacturing and textile industries, with the development of steam power for use in factories, shipping and rail transport that impacted social, cultural and economic life. Throughout that time, agriculture, manufacturing and trade were the major industries where labour was deployed in the United States.

Figure 34: Share of total employment by sector in the United States, 1850–2015 (per cent of jobs)

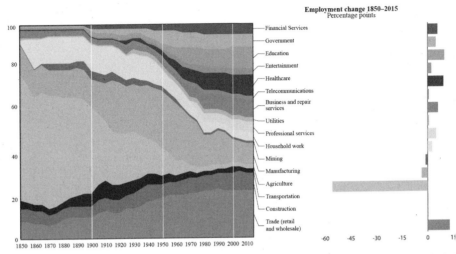

The Second Industrial Revolution (1870–1970), also referred to as the Technological Revolution, saw a period of rapid industrialisation in the latter part of the 19th century and beginning of the 20th century. The expansion of rail and telegraph lines enabled significant movement of people, ideas and trade. Revolutions in power, telecommunications, iron and steel opened up employment across trade, construction, mass manufacturing and expansion of services-based industries.

The Third Industrial Revolution (1970 to the present), in the second half of the 20th century, emerged with new types of energy: i.e. nuclear, solar, wind and geothermal. This revolution gave rise to transformational innovations associated with electronics and the microprocessor, telecommunications and computers, and biotechnology. High-level automation in production, thanks to inventions in programmable logic controllers and robotics, opened up employment in manufacturing, while information technology developments expanded employment across financial services, education, healthcare and trade.

The most significant changes to employment in the United States in the 165 years from 1850 to 2015 included declines in the importance of agriculture, manufacturing and mining. However, increases occurred across all other industries, especially trade, education, business and repair services and professional services. History does indeed demonstrate that labour markets adjust to changes in demand for labour from disruptive technological advancements.

What is different with this new round of automation advancement is that it is targeting most knowledge areas—for example, legal, accounting and financial services with 'robo advice'. What we can observe is that these adjustments were more frequent in the US from 1970 onwards than in any other previous period.

So, we need to rebalance our thinking toward such questions as: what new jobs will be required to support the next industrial revolution, and how do we reskill existing jobs and create new skills (and jobs) to support the future demand of labour?

As we saw in Chapter Four, Figure 25, an overwhelming number of Millennials (78 per cent) believe that technology will create jobs; so how can we leverage this confidence for future employment? But it's not just the workforce itself that we need to consider, but the very real possibility that we need to redefine the nature of work and its relationship to reward.

According to McKinsey, if history is any guide, 8–9 per cent of labour demand in 2030 will be in new types of occupations that have not existed before. They predict that by 2030, as many as 375 million workers, or approximately 14 per cent of the global workforce, may need to be reskilled as digitisation, automation and Artificial Intelligence technologies disrupt industries. They predict that with adequate economic growth and investment, there will be enough new jobs to offset those impacted by automation. Their analysis highlights that 60 per cent of existing occupations have more than 30 per cent of activities that can be automated technologically, illustrating the widespread impact of automation on existing occupations [62] (see Figure 35).

Katherine Johnson's remarkable life and contributions to society, science and computing were recognised with the Presidential Medal of Freedom in 2015. One of the key lessons we can take from her experience is that despite the introduction of in-memory computing that transformed calculating by hand, she adapted and worked directly with computers. The spirit of her story reflects humankind's ability to adapt and augment disruptive technological advancement.

As with each industrial revolution, the disruptive emerging technologies destroyed jobs where routine and repetitive tasks were mechanised, but created many new ones, shifting human

Figure 35: Automation and its impact on labour

Technical automation potential	**-50%** of current work activities are technically automatable by adapting currently demonstrated technologies		**6 of 10** current occupations have more than 30% of activities that are technically automatable	

		Slowest	Midpoint	Fastest
Impact of adoption by 2030	Work potentially displaced by adoption of automation by adoption scenario % of workers (FTEs[1])	0% (10 million)	15% (400 million)	30% (800 million)
	Workforce that could need change occupational category, by adoption scenario,[2] % of workers (FTEs)	Slowest 0% (<10 million)	Midpoint 3% (75 million)	Fastest 14% (375 million)

		Low		High
Impact of demand for work by 2030 from 7 select trends[3]	Trending demand scenario % of workers (FTEs)	15% (390 million)		22% (590 million)
	Step-up demand scenario % of workers (FTEs)	5% (165 million)		11% (300 million)
	Total, % of workers (FTEs)	21% (555 million)		33% (890 million)

In addition, of the 2030 workforce of 1.66 billion, 8–9% will be now in new occupations[4]

1 Full-time equivalent
2 In trendline labour-demand scenario
3 Rising incomes; healthcare from aging; investment in technology, infrastructure and buildings; energy transitions; and marketisation of unpaid work. Not exhaustive.
4 See Jeffreyy Lin, "Technological adaptation, cities and work", *Review of Economics and Statistics*, Volume 93, Number 2, 2011.

capital to higher value-adding activities. The widespread innovation of the technological revolution created new industries and jobs that didn't exist pre-1970.

Because the Fourth Industrial Revolution runs on knowledge, we need a concurrent revolution in training and education. Here, both government and business must join forces to provide workers with the skills and qualifications they need to participate in the digital economy.

— Joe Kaeser
president and CEO of Siemens AG

So, what are the attributes that influence Millennials' choice of careers or employment? The top three most important criteria when considering job opportunities are salary/financial compensation, sense of purpose/impact on society, and growth/career advancement (see Figure 36).

Figure 36: What are your most important criteria when considering job opportunities? (per cent) (N=20070)

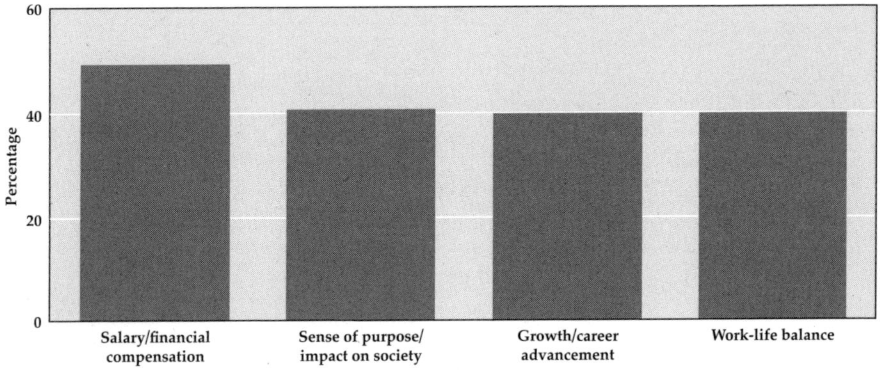

Percentage of unique votes. Respondents were allowed to choose up to three answer choices.
Next leading choices were "Flexibility/autonomy" (28.1%), "Company culture/quality of colleagues" (26.0%)

Source: WEF Global Shapers Survey 2017
Reproduced by permission

As discussed in Chapter Three, there is a significant and widening gap between Millennials' expectations of the role of organisations as a force for positive change, and their perceived current performance. This may explain Millennials' attraction to emerging organisations that have a transformational purpose. Examples of such organisations are listed in Table 1:

Table 1

Organisation	Massive transformational purpose
Google	'Organise the world's information'
Singularity University	'Positively impact one billion people'
Uber	'To make transportation as reliable as running water, everywhere for everyone'
Ant Financial	'To collaborate with local partners through technology transfer, to make services more accessible'
Amazon	'To be Earth's most customer-centric company, where customers can find and discover the lowest prices'

Annexed to Amazon's massive transformational purpose is its employees' purpose.

We pioneer

We're a company of pioneers. It's our job to make bold bets, and we get our energy from inventing on behalf of our customers. Success is measured against the possible, not probable. For today's pioneers, that's exactly why there's no place on Earth they'd rather be.

— **Amazon**

Millennials see work as part of their lives rather than something separate. It is intertwined with how they identify themselves. This is a significant change from older generations, who compartmentalised their lives: 'I have my home over here, my work life over there, and I have my social life up in the air.' For example, 42.1 per cent of Millennials expect it should be part of their employer's mandate to ensure work/life balance (see Figure 37).

Figure 37: Which one of the following descriptions come closest to your attitude towards work-life balance? (N=20034)

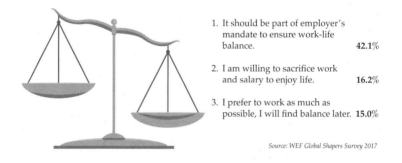

1. It should be part of employer's mandate to ensure work-life balance.   **42.1%**

2. I am willing to sacrifice work and salary to enjoy life.   **16.2%**

3. I prefer to work as much as possible, I will find balance later.   **15.0%**

Source: WEF Global Shapers Survey 2017

Interestingly, the age variation for the option 'I am willing to sacrifice work and salary to enjoy life' with those aged 31–35 years (18.5 per cent) to those aged 18–24 years (13.4 per cent) highlights the life stage differences between those groups. The opposite is also true for 'I prefer to work as much as possible, I will find balance later' with 31–35 year olds (12.2 per cent) compared to those aged 18–24 years 17.5 per cent.

Unlike generations before them where their neighbourhood was their locality, to Millennials the world is their neighbourhood. As the most diverse generation ever, they enjoy the cultural richness that multiculturalism has provided. This translates directly into their views on careers. A truly global generation,

Figure 38: Would you be willing to live outside your country of residence in order to find a job or advance your career? (N=20049)

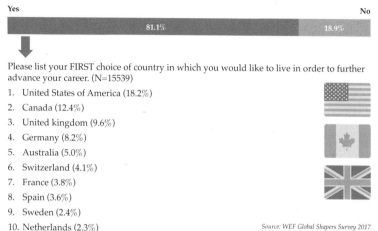

Yes   No

| 81.1% | 18.9% |

Please list your FIRST choice of country in which you would like to live in order to further advance your career. (N=15539)

1. United States of America (18.2%)
2. Canada (12.4%)
3. United kingdom (9.6%)
4. Germany (8.2%)
5. Australia (5.0%)
6. Switzerland (4.1%)
7. France (3.8%)
8. Spain (3.6%)
9. Sweden (2.4%)
10. Netherlands (2.3%)

Source: WEF Global Shapers Survey 2017

their willingness to work outside their home country is an astounding 83 per cent 'yes' (see Figure 38).

How nations, industries and organisations develop their human capital can be a more important determinant of their long-term success than virtually any other factor. The ability to attract, retain and grow Millennial human capital will be critical, because of their openness to progress their careers outside their country of residence.

In its annual benchmarking study, which measures and ranks 119 countries and 90 cities based on their ability to grow, attract and retain talent, GTCI[63] in its 2018 report, found that countries are competing globally to grow better talent; attract the talent they need; and retain those workers who contribute to competitiveness, innovation, and growth. They found that countries were seeking to put economic and social policies in place to facilitate this. The top 10 countries for talent competitiveness were Switzerland, Singapore, USA, Norway, Sweden, Finland, Denmark, UK, Netherlands, and Luxembourg. The top 10 cities were Zurich, Stockholm, Oslo, Copenhagen, Helsinki, Washington, D.C., Dublin, San Francisco, Paris and Brussels. These nations and cities are well aligned with the desirability of Millennials to progress their careers.

Technology is not the only factor that Millennials overwhelmingly believe will create jobs. Businesses also have an important role to play. The most important contribution that business makes to society is to 'create jobs' (30.5 per cent), 'improve livelihoods' (20.7 per cent) and 'boosting the economy' (14.6 per cent) (see Figure 39).

Figure 39: What do you consider to be most important contribution that businesses make to society? (N=18857)

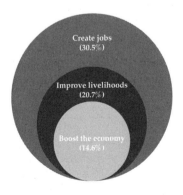

Source: WEF Global Shapers Survey 2017

This reflects the expectation of companies to get involved and address social and environmental problems. In fact, 66 per cent disagreed with the statement 'Companies should not be involved in addressing social problems that are not related to their business activities'—which correlates to the insight that young adults seek meaning and purpose in the work they do.

So, what can businesses do to create a youth-friendly culture in the workplace? As discussed in Chapter Three (see Figure 15), Millennials feel they have the least influence on the strategic direction of the organisation, so see this as the biggest opportunity to contribute to the organisation's vision and strategy (see Figure 40).

Figure 40: How do you decide whether a company is responsible or not? (per cent) (N=19826)

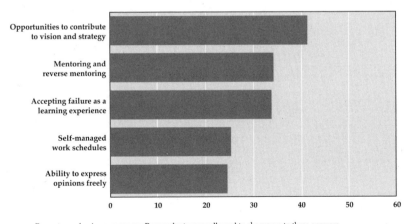

Percentage of unique responses. Respondents were allowed to choose up to three answers.
Following answer choices are *Engage young board members* (22.5%), *Allotting time for person projects* (17.7%)

Source: WEF Global Shapers Survey 2017

This highly-educated, connected and values-driven generation, will do as much, if not more, due diligence on organisations they may be interested in working for, than organisations do on them. The reputation of an organisation will be critical in their considerations, particularly on whether it is socially responsible or not. They will draw upon a wide range of publicly available information for their assessment (see Figure 41). Importantly, as discussed in Chapter Five, they will rely on independent, reputable institutions as sources of that information.

Figure 41: How do you decide whether a company is responsible or not? (per cent) (N=19826)

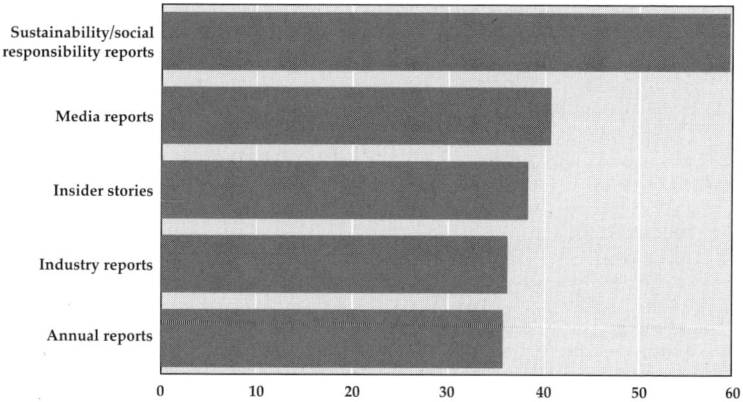

Percentage of unique votes. Respondents were allowed to choose as many answers choices as applicable. Next leading choices are *Online article* (commentary" (30.7%), *Friends/network* (26.9%)

Source: WEF Global Shapers Survey 2017

Gender diversity

There are many arguments on how gender diversity enhances society. But the most rational one is quite simple. Without diversity and inclusion, organisations underperform and ultimately fail, because of their inability to optimise female human capital. The more gender diverse an organisation is, the more profit it makes. Simple as that.

Globally, gender inequality is a major moral, social and economic challenge. Millennials, who thrive on digital, empowerment and inclusion, will be the first generation to correct the inequalities that generations before them either haven't or were unwilling to address. But let me be clear: I do acknowledge the tremendous efforts of those from other generational groups spearheading change. Thank you for your courage and leadership. And while we have made progress in recent years with women's representation as leaders improving in many parts of the world, women are far from achieving equality.

We simply cannot reflect on the past three industrial revolutions without considering the tremendous opportunity gender equality offers us in the Fourth Industrial Revolution. Women make up half of the world's population and workforce, yet they don't achieve their full economic potential. As I discussed earlier, the world has only developed 62 per cent of its human capital leaving 38 per cent underutilised, a large proportion of which are women. According to a McKinsey report, gender equality could add US$12 trillion or 11 per cent to global GDP by 2025[64]. In a full potential scenario, this could sky-rocket to US$28 trillion or 26 per cent of global GDP by 2025. Now there are not many initiatives addressing global challenges that offer that quantum payload.

Figure 42: Concentration of women by sector

		Average productivity[2] 2014, index agriculture =1	Female-male share of employment[3] % of total female employment minus that of male	Female share of employment[3] % of total female employment
Agriculture	Agriculture	1	-1	2
Industry	Mining and quarrying	21	-2	1
	Utilities	9	-1	1
	Manufacturing	3	-2	21
	Construction	2	-12	3
Services	Financial intermediation	8	2	4
	Real estate, renting and business activities	7	-1	7
	Public administration and defence	4	-2	8
	Transport, storage and communications	3	-3	3
	Wholesale and retail trade	2	1	11
	Health and social work	2	9	12
	Education	2	8	14
	Hotels and restaurants	1	2	5
	Other services	1	3	6

1 Australia, Brazil, Canada, China, Italy, Japan, Mexico, Netherland, Russia, Saudi Arabia, South Korea, Spain, Sweden, Turkey, United States
2 Sample average
3 Weighted average

According to McKinsey's analysis across 17 countries, women currently generate approximately 37 per cent of global GDP, which is significantly lower than their 50 per cent population representation. Women are also disproportionately represented in lower-productivity industry sectors when evaluating their GDP contribution per worker (see Figure 42 for examples in industries such as education and healthcare). Women tend to be concentrated in the service sector, rather than the industrial sector, which has a higher average productivity.

Leadership is the key, specifically gender-diverse leadership. In another major study across 91 countries analysing 21,980 publicly traded companies, The Peterson Institute for International

Economics and EY[65] shows that organisations with 30 per cent female leaders could add up to six per cent in net margin. The research indicates that while increasing the number of female representatives on boards and in CEO positions is important, increasing the number of female C-suites would likely benefit profit even more. Despite the positive correlation between C-level female representation and economic performance, the study revealed the magnitude of change required. For example:

- One third of companies globally have no women in either board or C-suite positions
- 60 per cent have no female board members
- 50 per cent have no female top executives
- Only five per cent have a female CEO

Figure 43: Proportion of women employees and representation of women in management by Australian industry

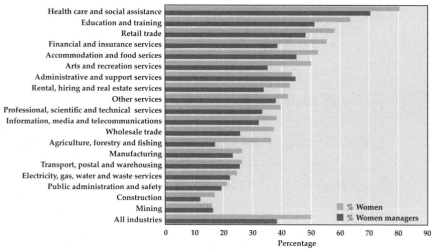

Source: Workplace Gender Equality Agency
Reproduced by permission

At an industry level, the concentration of women in management varies significantly. A 2017 study by the Australian Government's Workplace Gender Equality Agency[66] found that just seven of 19 industries have at least 40 percent women in management. Women were found to be most concentrated in the healthcare and social assistance sectors, and least represented in the construction and mining sectors (see Figure 43). When we analyse the proportion of women across those industries and the corresponding proportion of women as managers, there are significant gaps, particularly in the following sectors: agricultural, forestry and fishing (19.4 per cent); financial and insurance (16.9 per cent); and arts and recreation (14.7 per cent).

So what does it take to increase female representation? Research by Deloitte in 2017[67] revealed that diversity and inclusion has become a CEO-level priority, with an increasing proportion of executives citing diversity and inclusion as a top priority.

Increased corporate transparency, together with community and stakeholder awareness, has put the spotlight on many organisations' diversity and inclusion activities, elevating its priority and impact on brand, performance, and employee engagement. Investors are now becoming attuned to the increasing body of research that demonstrates how diversity and inclusion is becoming a lead indicator for organisational performance.

Companies that are executing robust human capital strategies based on diversity and inclusion are outperforming their peers, generating up to 30 per cent higher revenue per employee and greater profitability than competitors[68]. While training initiatives on topics such as bias are helpful, interventions and structural change are also important to accelerate change. What gets measured gets done right—so increasing the focus on measurement through key objectives and leadership accountability is where progressive organisations' policy settings are heading. In countries like Australia, the State Government of Victoria is experimenting with removing all personal information on job applications in blind tests designed to remove all bias[69].

Other organisations are taking a data-led approach by comparing job classes by gender, searching for either parity or inequality and publicly reporting their performance. Energy Australia, a leading utilities organisation, announced that women would be paid the same as male colleagues for doing the same job. The company announced that it would spend AUD$1.2 million to close the pay gap for 350 women who were paid less than their male counterparts for doing the same job. Managing director Catherine Tanna said: 'I am really pleased that we're able to say this year, 2018, at Energy Australia, we're bridging that gap. … But I'm sorry that it's taken so long and that our women at Energy Australia have had to wait so long.'[70] Ms Tanna said she hoped the company's move would set a good example for other employers.

For Millennials, diversity and inclusion are critical factors in deciding which organisations their values and beliefs align to—and which ones they won't work for. To them, diversity and inclusion performance demonstrates that an organisation's culture fosters innovation, engagement and teamwork, as well as values such as respect, integrity and responsibility. Often, they'll compare the stated values of an organisation and its diversity and inclusion metrics when deciding whether to join or leave a company. With this demographic, we will likely see a much greater proportion of dual income families, where both partners will expect equal treatment and pay.

According to research by Deloitte,[71] there is a significant gap in the workplace between what Millennials define as inclusion and what they define as diversity, compared to non-Millennials. To Millennials, inclusion means a collaborative environment that values open participation from individuals with different ideas and perspectives and unique factors of their personalities and behaviours. This is in contrast to non-Millennials, who define it as representation and assimilation (see Table 2).

Table 2: Definition of Inclusion

Millennials	Non-Millennials
28 per cent more likely to focus on business impact	28 per cent more likely to focus on fairness of opportunity
71 per cent more likely to focus on teamwork	31 per cent more likely to focus on equality
22 per cent more likely to focus on culture of connection	26 per cent more likely to focus on integration
	28 per cent more likely to focus on acceptance and tolerance

Source: Deloitte

Millennials define diversity as it relates to the individual mix of unique experiences, identities, ideas and opinions. Non-Millennials, by contrast, define diversity in terms of demographics, equal opportunity, representation and identifiable characteristics (see Table 3).

Table 3: Definition of Diversity

Millennials	Non-Millennials
32 per cent more likely to focus on respecting identities	21 per cent more likely to focus on representation
35 per cent more likely to focus on unique experiences	19 per cent more likely to focus on religion and demographics
29 per cent more likely to focus on ideas, opinions, thoughts	25 per cent more likely to focus on equality

Source: Deloitte

Unsurprisingly, inclusion impacts the level of engagement. For example, the study revealed that when they believe the organisation fosters an inclusive culture, 83 per cent of Millennials are actively engaged, as opposed to 60 per cent when they don't feel the organisation fosters an inclusive culture. As outlined in Chapter One, to Millennials, empowerment is not selfishly defined; it's about empowering others to succeed. They report much higher levels of empowerment when in inclusive cultures (76 per cent). In Chapter Three, I also outlined how their work is intertwined with their life, and so Millennials also report significantly higher levels of authenticity when operating in an inclusive culture (81 per cent), compared to when they are not (59 per cent).

Figure 44: Youth (15–30 years) unemployment rate, 2000–2016

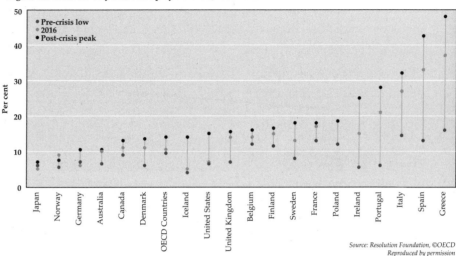

Source: Resolution Foundation, ©OECD
Reproduced by permission

Youth unemployment

Another major aspect of diversity as it relates to Millennials is their workforce participation. When we compare OECD countries, we see a significant spread of unemployment pre-2007 financial crisis (in 2000) compared to 2016[72] (see Figure 44). While the average rate among OECD countries shows that youth unemployment rose by less than four per cent compared to pre-crisis lows, youth unemployment more than doubled from 15 per cent to 30 per cent in Italy, Spain and Greece between 2000 and 2008. In the UK, youth unemployment was at nine per cent in 2016, at about the same level as in 2000.

As unemployment rates can fluctuate when people leave the labour market, participation rates that include employed or unemployed are an important measure of the extent to which Millennials are active in the labour market.

Figure 45: Youth (15–30 years) labour market participation rate, 2000–2016

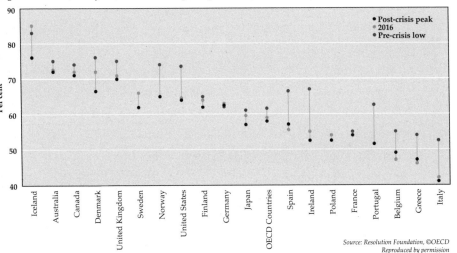

Source: Resolution Foundation, ©OECD
Reproduced by permission

We can see in Figure 45 the stark difference between the participation rates of countries such as Iceland, where some 80 per cent of Millennials participate in the economy, and at the opposite end of that spectrum, Italy, where 40 per cent of Millennials are economically active. This analysis also highlights a correlation between countries where youth unemployment has increased and participation rates declined.

In this chapter I've considered how adaptable human capital has been over the past three industrial revolutions and shifted our thinking to examine what skills will require redeploying or developing to ensure we meet the demands of the new economic reality.

Purpose is critical to Millennials, not only for alignment of values, but because they see what they do in life as being intertwined with who they are, and they are willing to look beyond their home country in pursuit of that goal.

Competition for labour, therefore, with this demographic is no longer a domestic issue, but a global one. The most significant underestimation of organisations is the role of gender and demographic diversity and inclusive human capital. How can we claim we've optimised all that the Third Industrial Revolution had to offer when the evidence suggests that a third of companies globally have no women in either board or C-suite positions—when we know that organisations with 30 per cent female leaders could add up to six per cent in net margin? Globally, gender diversity has the potential to add between US$12–28 trillion, or 11–25 per cent of global GDP by 2025. Now there are not too many initiatives to address global challenges that offer that quantum of payload.

For Katherine Johnson, it took the courage, conviction and belief in her by the composite of Al Harrison (played by Kevin Costner) and others at NASA Langley Research Centre to break down the barriers to racial and gender inequality and inclusion. Closing the gap takes leadership.

When we talk about feminism (she describes as
another expression of equality) and women's rights,
we're actually addressing men and we want them
to recognize that women should be accepted.

— **Malala Yousafzai**
youngest Nobel Prize Laureate

Chapter summary

- History shows labour markets have adapted to disruptions that occurred in the First, Second, and Third Industrial Revolutions. The question should be centered on what new jobs will be needed in the Fourth Industrial Revolution and how we reskill the necessary pools of labour to meet the demands.

- By 2030, it is predicted that approximately 14 per cent of the global workforce (approximately 375 million workers) will be required to be reskilled.

- We need to rebalance our thinking to examine what new skills will be required for the future and how we reskill redundant labour and create new jobs.

- When considering job opportunities, the 'sense of purpose, impact on society and career growth advancements' will be critical factors for Millennials in deciding who to work for, in addition to salary and financial compensation.

- A truly global generation, 81 per cent of Millennials would be willing to live outside their country of residence in order to advance their careers, with the US, Canada, UK, Germany and Australia among the top five destinations.

- Millennials see the creation of jobs as being the most important contribution businesses can make to society, and involving them in contributing to the creation of an organisation's vision and strategy is the most important way to create a youth-friendly culture.

- Millennials seek meaning and purpose in the work they do; 66 per cent disagreed with the statement 'Companies should not be involved in addressing social problems that are not related to their business activities'.

- The reputation of the organisation and its social responsibility will be critical factors that will influence their choice of employer.

- Without diversity and inclusion, organisations underperform and ultimately fail, due to their inability to optimise female human capital. The more gender diverse an organisation is, the more profit it makes.

- Globally, gender diversity has the potential to add between US$12–28 trillion, or 11–26 per cent of global GDP by 2025.

- Youth unemployment is another major global challenge. There is a correlation between countries where youth unemployment has increased and participation rates declined.

- For Millennials, inclusion means a collaborative environment that values open participation from individuals with different ideas and perspectives.

- Millennials define diversity as it relates to the individual mix of unique experiences, identities, ideas and opinions.

- Inclusion impacts levels of engagement—83 per cent of Millennials are actively engaged if they believe the organisation fosters an inclusive culture.

- Millennials feel significantly higher levels of authenticity when operating in an inclusive culture (81 per cent).

Chapter Seven

FROM THE QUARTER-LIFE CRISIS TO JUVENESCENCE

We're here for a good time, and a long time

> *If I have the belief that I can do it, I shall*
> *surely acquire the capacity to do it, even if*
> *I may not have it at the beginning.*

— Plato
The Republic

The most precious, irreplaceable resource we have is time, and this resource has been increasing through life expectancy at a rate of two years every decade for the past 200 years[73]. This increase has followed a linear trajectory since 1840.

Becoming a centenarian is a very special experience, today achieved by less than one per cent of people born 100 years ago. But a child born in the developed world today has a more than 50 per cent chance of living to be over 105 years. If you are a Millennial aged 20, you have a 50 per cent chance of living to 100 years or more. This scarcest of resources (time) has become more abundant for Millennials than any other generation. Not only do we now need to consider the pace of change itself, but also, importantly, how longevity will impact society, economies, businesses and industries—for this is happening today.

The key question for us to consider in this chapter is: how will Millennials structure this surplus time?

In this chapter, I'll draw upon the wonderful insights of Lynda Gratton and Andrew Scott's book *The 100-Year Life: Living and Working in an Age of Longevity*[74], which was shortlisted for business book of the year in 2016, and consider the implications that longevity will have in the way Millennials approach life.

How was time structured in the twentieth century?

In the past, our lives were primarily organised around a linear three-stage model. First, came education that varied significantly for each generation; second, we entered the workforce and where, up to the 1980s, our expectations centred on lifelong employment (often with the same organisation); and last came retirement. With populations ageing, today many governments and citizens are coming to the realisation that this model is not sustainable.

This model has outlived its usefulness for a range of reasons, including longevity, demand for more labour, mobility and globalisation. To maintain this linear model, the only options are for people to either work longer, save more, or retire with a lower quality of life—which is why we need to think differently about how we structure our time, the definition of work and its relationship to reward. Today's leaders need to diligently pursue the long and uncomfortable discourse that will pave the way for a model that makes sense in a Millennial world.

It is important to not confuse postponing major life stages with lack of desire. Contrary to popular commentary, delaying marriage, home ownership, or starting families later than previous generations doesn't mean Millennials aren't interested in these life events. In fact, according to a 2017 study of 1,716 people aged between 25–75 by the Stanford Centre on Longevity[75], researchers found that in the US, the desired timing of those milestones remained relatively consistent across generations (see Figure 46). Researchers found that those milestones have successively declined for all generations. Although Millennials are the least likely to achieve these milestones, the study found that they ideally wanted to marry

Figure 46: Proportion of Americans achieving milestones by ideal age (per cent)

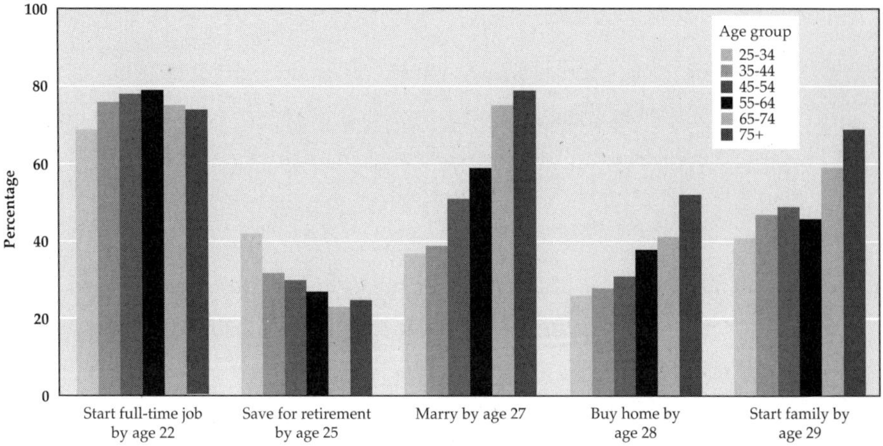

Source: Stanford University Study on Longevity
Reproduced by permission

by 27 years of age, buy a home by 28 years and start a family by 29 years. As discussed in Chapter Two, in those countries such as the US, UK and Australia, student debt has had a significant impact on these life stages, resulting in their deferment.

The three-stage model of education, employment and retirement simply won't accommodate Millennials' futures, nor those of generations that follow them as life expectancy increases; while at the same time, longevity is rapidly decreasing for organisations, and indeed industries, as I'll expand upon in Chapter Eight. The average lifespan of Fortune 500 companies reportedly decreased from 60 years in the 1920s to 15 years today. Forty per cent of Fortune 500 companies are predicted not to survive the next 10 years[76]. Researchers have been predicting these adjustments for some time. This generation's 'flexibility' and organisations' 'agility' will be critical for changes to these transitions. The key point here is that the past cannot be a reliable predictor of our employment future.

The significance of this surplus time can be thought of as follows. Today, life expectancy at birth exceeds 80 years on average in OECD countries (an increase of more than 10 years since 1970)[77] (see Figure 47).

The OECD reports that healthier lifestyles, higher incomes and better education have contributed to the increase in life expectancy in recent decades. In a study of 35 OECD countries, they predict that life expectancy gains of approximately eight years could be expected, through a doubling of heath care spending, doubling

Figure 47: Life expectancy at birth 1970 and 2015 (or nearest year)

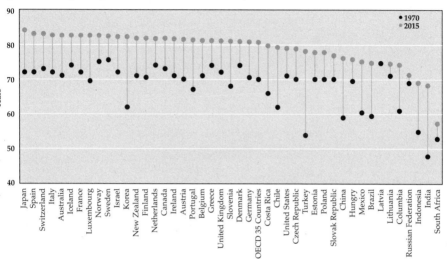

Source: ©OECD

income, reaching 100 per cent tertiary education and halving smoking and alcohol consumption (see Figure 48). This illustrates the economic sustainability dilemma facing governments and citizens, suggesting a 2.5x public, private or hybrid investment requirement across these critical services to support a 100-year life expectancy.

Rising life expectancy, together with declining birth rates in most OECD countries, creates an old age dependency profile described as the number of people of retirement age as a percentage of those of employment age. Over the next 50 years, the world average is predicted to double (see Figure 49), significantly impacting the investment required by governments in the areas of health, education, employment and welfare/pensions to significantly increase relative to GDP.

Figure 48: Life expectancy predicted gains based on analysis of 35 OECD Countries (1995–2015)

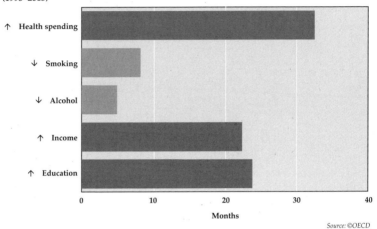

Source: ©OECD

Figure 49: Life expectancy at birth for the world and regions (1950–2050)

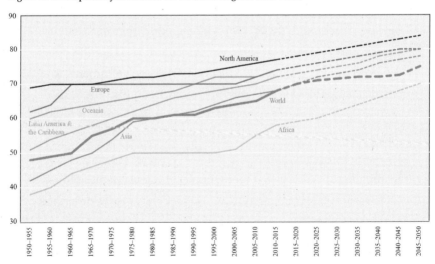

Source: United Nations (2015). World Population Prospects: The 2015

For example, in Australia, this increase has been estimated to be 21 per cent of GDP in 1990, increasing to 24 per cent in 2051[78]. Governments across the OECD are accordingly raising the retirement age for both women and men between 2010–2050[79]. This raises significant policy challenges for governments as they seek to reconcile the interests of influential older voters with Millennial voters.

I should note that an ageing population not only presents policy challenges for governments and businesses, but also creates enormous opportunities, as older people are a valuable asset. They embody a wealth of knowledge, experience and skills that are invaluable to society economically, socially and culturally.

How might time be structured in the 21st century?

There is never a straight line to success,
and there wasn't for me.

— **Sir Elton John**
musician and Crystal Award winner

Our lives will require a fundamental redesign to become multi-staged to accommodate a 100-year life. Distribution of this surplus time by 'extending of our working lives' is simplistic and not a plausible (or a desirable) solution. It doesn't reconcile with a world where the pace of change is now exponential and no longer linear. It also doesn't consider how time could be distributed across our leisure and family time.

Becoming 'agile' should not be limited to how we operate organisationally, but 'resilient agility' might be how we live individually. We are witnessing this among Millennials, who are keeping their life options open: delaying the transition to student life by often taking a gap year; from student life to professional life, by travelling abroad; and from single life into family life, by pursuing other lifestyle choices. This is a time of experimentation for them.

As Gratton & Scott suggest in their book, *The 100 Year Life*, re-creation with new life stages requires investment in shifting identity to take on new roles, different lifestyles or the development of new skills. We are likely to move away from age-related life stages to age-agnostic stages. This misalignment between the two models and its impact on expectations and the notion of 'success' was well articulated by 28-year-old Sally White in her 2017 TEDx presentation, 'Quarter-Life Crisis: Defining Millennial Success' (see Sally's story below)[80]. A quarter-life crisis is defined by the University of London as 'a commitment or set of commitments within a life structure that is no longer desired, yet not perceived as a realistic target of change'.

As many as 60 per cent of Millennials in the UK[81] are reported to go through a quarter-life crisis. In a study of 2000 British Millennials commissioned by First Direct Bank and psychologist Dr Oliver Robinson, 53 per cent were struggling to cope with financial pressures, 26 per cent struggling with careers, 22 per cent struggling with trying to get into the property market, and 25 per cent struggling with personal pressures in finding a satisfying relationship. The study revealed that it took an average of six months before they recovered, highlighting that there may not be short-term solutions in how this crisis is dealt with. However, Dr Robinson indicated, 'there were two sides to a quarter-life crisis. … They're often feared as periods of difficulty and distress, but in my experience, they can also be times of openness, curiosity and growth.'

In a separate study by LinkedIn of 1,001 Australian 25–33 year olds[82], as many as 80 per cent felt pressure to succeed before the age of 30. For Australian Millennials, the number one trigger for a quarter-life crisis was anxiety over finding a job or career path about which they felt passionately (64 per cent), and a staggering 29 per cent regretted that they wasted too many years in the wrong job. The next major triggers were finding a partner (44 per cent) or getting into the property market (49 per cent).

Sally's story

At the age of 23, Sally had 'climbed the corporate ladder, ticking all the boxes to becoming a responsible and successful adult'. However, this 'success' led to maintaining a lifestyle that was unsustainable, resulting in subsequent illness and marking the beginning of her quarter-life crisis. Her parents taught her that success would come from a good education, followed by a good job, marriage and then retirement. The classic three-stage linear model, with the promise of stability and security along the way. Sally's story illustrates how this model is inadequate for the Millennial generation. In her words:

We don't want work-life balance, we want work-life integration.

We want flexibility, sustainability, purpose and intrinsic motivations.

We want a life where our social interactions, personal wellness, and creative ambitions are intertwined to create a positive impact.

In a 100-year life, creative success needs to shape individual identity and be redesigned to develop the model through individual self-actualisation.

Longevity, as described by Gratton & Scott, is associated with ageing; however, they propose that there are powerful forces that will keep us younger for longer, referred to by Robert Pogue Harrison as *juvenescence*—the state of youthfulness. (The burgeoning cosmetics, cosmetic surgical, health and fitness industries are examples of this impulse.) Gratton & Scott introduce three new stages: the explorer, the independent producer and the portfolio, to describe how multi-stage, age-agnostic life stages may transpire. Let's examine how they apply to the Millennial generation.

The explorer

This stage of life is about exploring, travelling, seeking adventure and finding new experiences. It's about discovering what is out there, what they like and dislike and what they're good at. It's a time of experimentation and discovery and a period of *option creation* and seeking to make the right match at the right time— whether it is leisure, career, family or something else. Remember, their Baby Boomer parents rushed into these decisions and broke records along the way for their folly. While there have always been explorers at any time in life, there are three periods when this outlook fits best: 18–30 years, mid 40s, and 70–80 years.

While recovering from her quarter-life crisis, Sally White reflected on the negative impact of the long hours her colleagues were working and realised she 'didn't want that (life)' for herself. So she quit her corporate role, left Australia, moved to London and became an actress. For Sally, knowing what she didn't want was as important as knowing what she wanted. To illustrate the importance of this explorer stage, Sally explains: 'Changing your career path doesn't mean you're giving up … you don't have to be a slave to routine, that's a choice—so eat your avocado on toast.'

An independent producer

Entrepreneurship has given rise to a new stage of economic development. We saw in Chapter One that entrepreneurship is the most important factor to empowerment. There has never been a better time to consider an alternative to the conventional career path and start up a business. Technology advancements, access to capital, networks and skills have all lowered the barriers for start-ups. This desire exists for two-in-three Millennials, and is actually pursued by one-on-three Millennials today. This life stage is not just confined to Millennials; people can become independent producers at any age. Age is not a barrier to the success of start-ups. Many studies, such as that of Vivek Wadhwa at the Kauffman Foundation, Duke University, found that the average entrepreneur is 40 years old when they launch, with the average age of a successful start-up owner with over US$1 million in revenue 39 years[83].

This life stage involves creating jobs, rather than finding them, and is characterised by learning, building expertise and producing. This life stage exhibits greater risk that can result in failure, which has become an important aspect of experimentation and innovation. But it also opens up a world of lifestyle choices that are unavailable through conventional career paths.

For Sally White, she knew moving abroad to pursue a career as an actress would be a path of trial and error, with the knowledge that only two per cent of actors are employed at any one time. In an attempt to counter the risk, she set up her own business as a secondary source of income. While both were seemingly risky endeavours, her openness to risk, failure and rejection has been key in enabling her to redefine success on her own terms.

The portfolio

This life stage is about the pursuit of a combination of activities undertaken simultaneously. This life stage provides for financial accumulation, exploring, vitality and stimulation, learning and, importantly, making a social contribution. Confidence in the pursuit of this life stage often begins with exploring ideas while still maintaining a full-time career. Accelerator hubs are filled with individuals clustered to learn, experiment, prototype, and hopefully commercialise their ideas.

The gig economy is a good example of the portfolio stage, and is part of a shifting cultural and business environment that also includes the sharing economy, the gift economy and the barter economy. It's characterised by a high degree of autonomy, payment by task, and short-term relationships. According to McKinsey research in 2016[84], 20–30 per cent of the working age population of the United States and 15 per cent in the European Union undertake independent work.

Now to close out this last life stage, let's go back to Sally White. As well as pursuing her dream to become an actress, singer and dancer, Sally also provides freelance consulting services, has established a communication company providing videography and marketing services, and is the co-director of a London-based IT consultancy. Indeed, she has a diversified portfolio.

As discussed earlier, for Millennials in a linear-based, life stage model, there are only two transitions—from education to employment and from employment to retirement. Multi-stage, age-agnostic models, on the other hand, are more concentric and follow exponential trajectories. Motivations for each inversion will vary widely. For example, for Sally White, her illness, along with her quarter-life crisis, and the realisation that she needed to redefine success and that she didn't want to work the long hours, formed the basis of her transition into the explorer stage, the independent producer stage and the portfolio stage. Her motivations were to recharge her health and wellness and to recreate herself by relocating to London, creating new networks and pursuing her portfolio.

One of the greatest challenges Sally sees for Millennials in re-engineering their notion of success is creating a new definition of what it means to have stability. For Baby Boomers, this was established through consistency in career, which not only provided their basic needs, but also many of their psychological and self-fulfilment needs. That model is not sustainable, nor desirable, in today's economic climate. For Millennials like Sally, they will be much more likely to achieve that stability through increasing entrepreneurship and diversification of their skill sets so that, in a 100-year life, they can afford 'mini retirements'.

Millennials are more aware of society's many challenges than previous generations and less willing to accept maximising shareholder value as a sufficient goal for their work. They are looking for a broader social purpose and want to work somewhere that has such a purpose.

— Michael Porter
professor, Harvard Business School

Chapter summary

- Life expectancy has been steadily increasing by two years each decade since 1840. Millennials aged 20 have a 50 per cent chance of living to 100 years and may well live in a four-generation family construct.

- Investment in healthcare, education and better lifestyle choices have been the primary reasons for increased life expectancy.

- While life expectancy has been increasing for people, it's been decreasing for organisations. The average lifespan of Fortune 500 companies reportedly decreased from 60 years in the 1920s to 15 years today. Forty per cent of the Fortune 500 are predicted not to survive the next 10 years.

- The traditional, linear life stage model of education, employment and retirement is unlikely to explain our future in a world that is exponentially changing, where life expectancy is increasing, and the survival of organisations is declining.

- We can expect to see a shift from an age-based, linear life stage model, to an age-agnostic, multi-stage exponential model that will be critical to understanding how this longevity will be structured.

- Juvenescence through life stages that includes exploring, becoming an independent producer and creating a portfolio may explain how this generation will approach recreation.

- For many Millennials, the quarter-life crisis will become the catalyst for adopting a multi-stage approach to the way they live.

- Triggers for this quarter-life crisis are primarily centered on expectations of success, a career and its progression, access to the property market and the establishment of relationships, partners and family.

- This quarter-life crisis, however, offers opportunities for openness, curiosity and growth.

Chapter Eight

THE DIGITAL REVOLUTION

*A world where neither age, nor size or reputation guarantee
you'll be around tomorrow*

*The last 10 years have been about building a world that is
mobile-first, turning our phones into remote controls for our
lives. But in the next 10 years, we will shift to a world that is
AI-first, a world where computing becomes universally available.*

— **Sundar Pichai**
CEO of Google

So far, I've considered how Millennials may use their influence democratically, economically, culturally and technologically, and their attitude towards major global challenges. I've also examined future trends and how they may impact the world. I've considered our current state of trust and identified that in order to address our increasingly digital lives, the existing model requires extending the topology to connect with multiple actors operating in a distributed manner. Within that context, we'll turn our attention to the organisational challenges associated with the Technology Revolution and what this means as we enter the Fourth Industrial Revolution.

There are still many industries and organisations that are yet to fully embrace all that the Third Industrial Revolution has to offer technologically. A performance gap has now emerged between those organisations that invested in digital transformations and are applying digital technologies and strategies, and those that are still competing in traditional ways. We begin this chapter by reflecting on the following question: what impact has the Third Industrial Revolution had on the digitalisation of industries and organisations?

According to a 2017 study by McKinsey[85], organisations still competing in traditional ways demonstrated lower rates of revenue and earnings growth than those already digitally transformed. Importantly, they found that this performance was tightly correlated with the level of digitalisation in their industries. Those organisations that were digitally transformed had incorporated digital into their business (technology, analytics, skills), their strategic decision-making (business model innovation) and their execution models.

Without digitisation, the study reports that respondents estimate a third of revenues were at risk of loss or cannibalisation in the next three years. The concentration of digitisation at an industry level results in declining profit and revenue pools. Interestingly, the study found that those organisations that are adopting digitisation and hold significant market share, are just as great a threat as disruptive entrants (see Figure 50).

The spread between the least-impacted industry (consumer packaged goods at 16 per cent) to the most impacted (telecommunications at 44 per cent) highlights that no industry is exempt from the impact of digitisation. However, industries that are information enabled, such as telecommunications, media and entertainment, retail banking and other financial services industries, are most exposed and impacted. Hold that thought, as I'll come back to it when I assess exponential performance.

If we use ratio analysis to consider the level of disruption remaining in industries by observing the extent of industry digitisation relative to industry revenue at risk (DTR) between industries, we uncover some fascinating insights. For example, only the high-tech (90 per cent), other financial services (90 per cent) and media and entertainment (83 per cent) industries are above the average DTR (83 per cent). Unsurprisingly, these were the industries initially most impacted by digital disruption and have responded accordingly. Industries that are yet to transform digitally and most exposed to disruption of their revenues are telecommunication (64 per cent), insurance (64 per cent) and retail (67 per cent), all well below the average DTR of 83 per cent. At a DTR of 79 per cent, retail banking remains considerably exposed, which may explain the significant level of financial technology investment in play worldwide.

McKinsey found that most respondents report having a digitlsation plan in place, but have only invested in it moderately. Investment in digital had only been proportional to current revenues earned—not to growth aspirations. This

Figure 50: Digitisation risk to revenue next three years

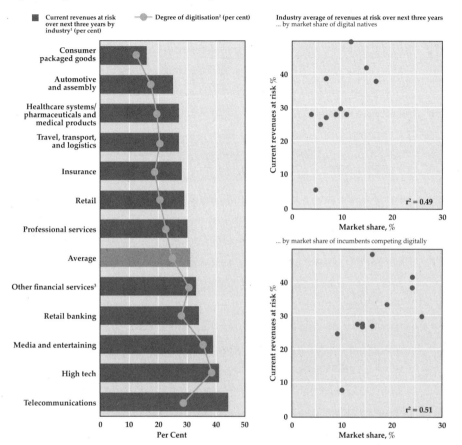

1 For consumer packed goods, n = 50; for automative and assembly, n = 68, for healthcare systems/pharmaceuticals and medical product, n = 101; for travel, transport, and logistics, n = 45; for insurance, n = 65; for retail, n = 72; for professional services, n = 247; for other financial services, n = 130; for retail banking, n = 60; for media and entertainment, n = 82; for high tech, n = 237; for telecommunications, n = 50.
2 Based on share of organisations' sales from products/services that are sold through digital channels; share of core products/services that are digital in nature (e.g. virtualised or digitally enhance); share of core operations automated and/or digitised; and share of volume in supply chain that is digitised or moved through digital interactions with suppliers.
3 Excludes respondents in insurance and retail banking.

underinvestment was pronounced in industries that stand to benefit most from disruptive technologies (see Figure 51). The high-tech industry is leading digitisation investment (revenue and workforce) followed by media and entertainment, then financial services—two industries well understood in terms of disruption.

When we analyse the ratio between the economic investment (revenue per cent) in digitalisation and the labour investment (workforce per cent) in digitalisation, we uncover more very interesting insights. Those investing less than 10 per cent of annual revenues on digital over the past three years (consumer packaged goods, insurance, automotive and assembly, retail) had an economic/human capital ratio ranging between 2.0–2.5, reflecting a greater reliance on labour in their digital transformations and developments. Those industries investing more than 11 per cent of annual revenues on digital over the past three years (healthcare systems, pharmaceutical and medical products, telecommunications, travel, transport and logistics, retail banking, other financial services, media and entertainment and high-tech) had an economic/human capital ratio of 2.0–1.1, reflecting a greater reliance on their economic investments to support their transformations and developments.

Again, we can see that information-enabled industries have a more balanced economic/human capital ratio, relative to manufacturing. The exception here is insurance, where compared to retail banking and other financial services it is 2x more reliant on labour investment for digital transformation and development.

Figure 51: Proportion of investment and people on digital initiatives, relative to revenue

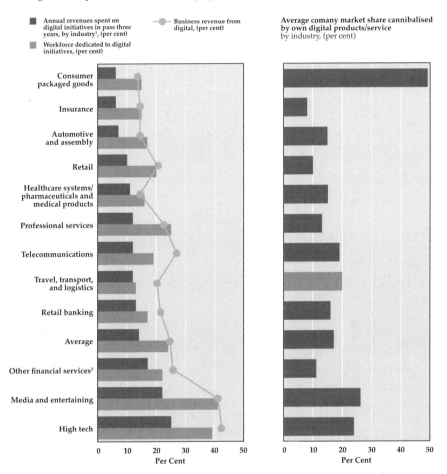

1 That is, compound annual—no total—revenue from sale of digital products and/or services, or revenues generated through digital channels. for consumer packaged goods, n = 50; for insurance, n = 65; for automative and assembly, n = 68; for retail, n = 72; for healthcare systems/pharmaceuticals and medical products, n = 101; for professional services, n = 247; for telecommunications, n = 50; for travel, transport, and logistics, n = 45; for retail banking, n = 60; for other financial services, n = 130; for media and entertainment, n = 82; for high tech, n = 237.
2 Respondents only were asked this question if they said they have launched digital versions of their products or services.
3 Excludes respondents in insurance and retail banking.

Source: Exhibit from "How digital reinvestors are pulling away from the pack", October 2017, McKinsey Global Institute, www.mckinsey.com. © 2018 McKinsey & Company. All rights reserved. Reprinted by permission.

The study did reveal that digital leaders and innovators exhibited common characteristics. These were:

1. **Business transformation.** They innovate their business models in a transformational way (as opposed to some incremental adjustments to strategy and core business).
2. **Scale up cutting-edge technologies.** They scale up cutting-edge technologies and techniques, applying design thinking at scale across the organisation or within business units.
3. **Decisive and significant investment.** They invest decisively and three times as much, and for the long term relative to traditional companies.
4. **Strategic context.** They see the world as interconnected ecosystems.

So, if the risk to revenues, profit or existence is well understood, where and why are strategies falling short on delivering enterprise value? The answer is often due to the irreconcilable economic, strategic and operational differences between their business-as-usual traditional model and the pace and scale of the disruptive transformational models. The pace of change in the external environment is moving faster than the organisation's capacity to adapt and respond. As Jack Welch so well-articulated:

If the rate of change on the outside exceeds the rate of change on the inside, the end is near...

Advancements in mobile technology illustrate this point. Consider the impact that smartphones have had in the way we communicate, shop and bank. It has been unarguably demonstrated to have disrupted the media, entertainment, retailing and financial services industries. As I outlined in Chapter Four, we are now living in a mobile media-first world, which connects 5.7 billion people. In such a relatively short period of time, approximately 10 years, the smartphone has become our gateway to the world and a primary mechanism for delivering personalisation. Yet despite this, there are many organisations that have not adapted their traditional models for this new mode of delivery. They took their business-as-usual model and simply put a thin, mobile veneer on it. This underestimation represents not only a lack of understanding of the behavioural change in habits from their customers, but also of the economic benefits that flow from digitisation.

Cloud and connectivity technology advancements are other examples where the traditional fixed-cost infrastructure model has struggled to adapt to the scalability and variability offered by those technologies through price/performance developments. Another consequence of the fixed-cost traditional infrastructure model is the labour intensity it requires to support it, inhibiting automation and scalability.

Despite the underestimations, according to McKinsey[86], only eight per cent of organisations believe their current business model would remain economically viable if their industry continues digitising at its current course. Their research identifies five explanations of why digital strategies are failing:

1. Lack of a clear, wholistic organisational definition of digital and its place in their business
2. Misunderstanding the economics of digital as it disaggregates value propositions, where economic rent becomes primarily redistributed in favour of customers
3. Understanding the new economic rules that digital will apply to the broader value chain as industries increasingly become ecosystems. The platformification of industries allows players to traverse across traditional boundaries that are increasingly becoming blurred
4. Overestimating digital attackers and underestimating the impact of a digitised incumbent with significant market share
5. Not digitising their traditional businesses and innovating with new models

The irony is that the results speak for themselves. Their research identified that first-movers and fast-followers with digital demonstrated a three-year revenue growth of over 12 per cent, which was nearly twice that of those companies with an average reaction to digital competition (see Figure 52).

So, are traditional organisations deriving value from their transformations?

The imperative to transform is now in full swing across developed markets. According to BCG analysis[87], 52 per cent of large public companies in Europe and North America announced transformations in 2016—a 42 per cent increase over

Figure 52: Don't underestimate how digital disrupts the nature of competition

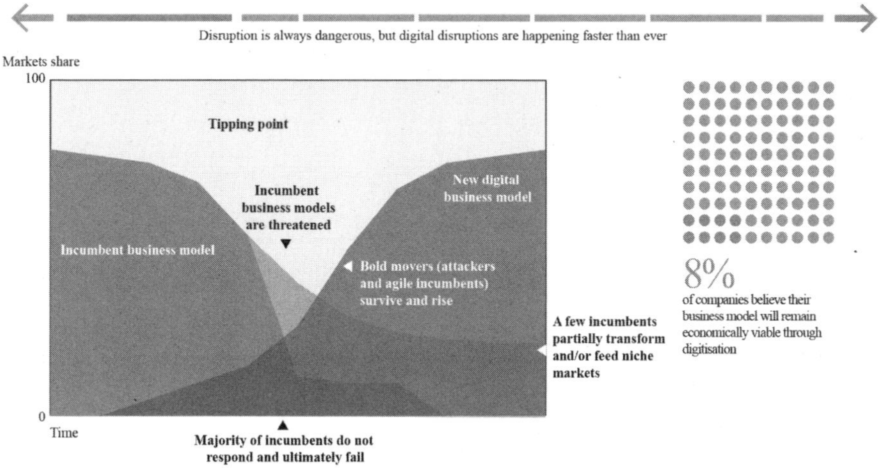
Disruption is always dangerous, but digital disruptions are happening faster than ever
Markets share
100
0
Time
Tipping point
Incumbent business models are threatened
New digital business model
Incumbent business model
Bold movers (attackers and agile incumbents) survive and rise
A few incumbents partially transform and/or feed niche markets
Majority of incumbents do not respond and ultimately fail
8%
of companies believe their business model will remain economically viable through digitisation

Source: Exhibit from "Why digital strategies fail", January 2017, McKinsey Global Institute, www.mckinsey.com. © 2018 McKinsey & Company. All rights reserved. Reprinted by permission.

the past 10 years. BCG's analysis sought to determine whether transformations were creating value by comparing the growth of total shareholder return (TSR) of transforming companies, with that of their respective industry. They discovered that only 24 per cent of transforming companies experienced greater TSG growth than their industry average over both the short term (one year), and the long term (five years plus) (see Figure 53).

Why are some organisations digitally outperforming others?

If you haven't transitioned into an Exponential Organization, it will not only seem as though your competition is racing away from you, but also like Kodak, that you are sliding backwards at breakneck speed.

— **Salim Ismail**
founding executive director, Singularity University

Figure 53: Value creation from transformations

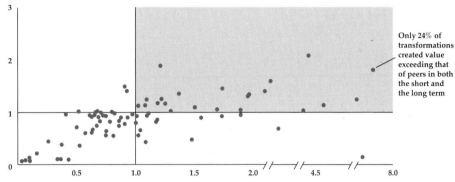

Long-term relative TSR growth

Relative TSR growth in year 1 of transformation

Only 24% of transformations created value exceeding that of peers in both the short and the long term

Note: TSR growth compared with S&P 500 or relevant global industry index growth, "1" equals same growth rate as the industry.
Long-term growth refers to a minimum five-year time frame. Sample of 88 large companies across sectors and geographies.
TSR = total shareholder return.

Source: Boston Consulting Group analysis
Reproduced by permission

Now let's turn our attention to 'exponential organisations' (ExOs) and understand why they are outperforming their competitors and then consider how prepared they are for this next revolution. Singularity University researchers have been leading insights in this field. They define an exponential organisation as one whose impact (or output) is disproportionately large—at least 10 times larger—compared to its peers, because of the use of new organisational techniques that leverage accelerating technologies[88].

Ismail, Malone and Van Geest in their book *Exponential Organizations: Why new organizations are ten times better, faster, and cheaper than yours* (2014), provide insights of the emergence of a new breed of organisation that leverages the power of platform-based, data-intensive and capital-light models designed with exponential technologies that scale for exponential, rather than linear, performance.

These organisations restructure value chains, taking what was once physical in nature and dematerialising it into the digital on-demand world; disaggregate processes separating them into components; and disintermediate by cutting out the non-value adding middleman. They have become leaders of the world's economy for the foreseeable future. These tech companies have taken over stock markets and in 2017, the top five were valued at US$3.3 trillion most (see Table 4).

Combined revenues from these tech companies rose to US$650 billion in 2017, and since 2002, have grown from 217 per cent to 27,625 per cent. As technology companies, however, most of their revenues are generated through very different product sets. For example, in 2017, 81 per cent of Apple's revenue was generated from hardware; for Google, 86 per cent from advertising; Microsoft, 62 per cent from software; Amazon, 82 per cent from retail; and Facebook, 98 per cent from advertising[89].

Table 4: Most valuable companies in the world by year by market capitalisation (US$B)

			■ Traditional company ■ Tech company		
Top	**2001** US $1,527bn	**2006** US$1,670bn	**2011** US$1,519bn	**2016** US$2,407bn	**2017** US$3,328bn
1	GE US$372bn	ExxonMobil US$447bn	ExxonMobil US$406bn	Apple US$609bn	Apple US$861bn
2	Microsoft US$327bn	GE US$383bn	Apple US$377bn	Google US$539bn	Google US$730bn
3	ExxonMobil US$300bn	Microsoft US$294bn	PetroChina US$275bn	Microsoft US$483bn	Microsoft US$600bn
4	Walmart US$273bn	citi US$274bn	Shell US$234bn	Berkshire Hathaway US$402bn	amazon US$564bn
5	citi US$255bn	Gazprom US$272bn	ICBC US$227bn	ExxonMobil US$374bn	Facebook US$513bn

Source: Morningtonstar; Financial Times; Statista

In his 30 years of research, Ray Kurzweil[90], a world-leading author, computer scientist, inventor, futurist and co-founder of the Singularity University, has made four key observations on exponential performance:

1. **The Multiplication effect**. Just like Moore's law theory of price/ performance of computation (where the transistor count doubles about every 18 months), this effect also applies to information technology. Kurzweil describes this as the 'law of accelerating returns'.
2. **Information enablement**. Once an industry, product or technology becomes information enabled, its price/performance doubles approximately every year.
3. **Acceleration**. Once doubling begins, it doesn't stop.
4. **Exponential technologies**. Information enabling technologies include Artificial Intelligence, robotics, biotech and bioinformatics, neuroscience, data science, 3D printing and nanotechnology.

These observations explain why technology and evolutionary processes progress in an exponential manner. These accelerating technologies enable the marginal cost of both supply and demand to reduce to virtually zero, delivering scale that previous linear-based models simply cannot achieve (see Figure 54).

Since 2014, we have witnessed a three times-plus surge in the number of exponential organisations reaching what is referred to as 'unicorn' status in their valuations (i.e., reaching US$1 billion)[91] (see Figure 55). Investors believe these companies have platforms and products of the future, and place big bets on them—but we

Figure 54: Exponential versus linear performance

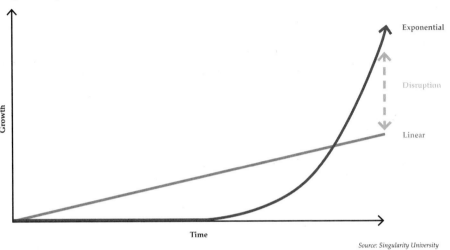

Source: Singularity University

Figure 55: Number of startups with US$1 billion+ valuation by year

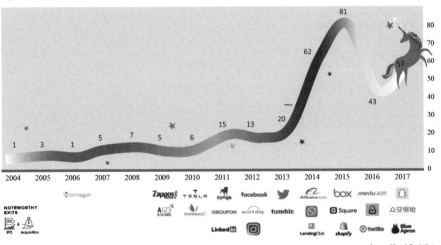

Source: Visual Capitalist

must note, not all unicorns survive. This has become the new environment in which organisations must operate. The scale and impact of disruption is now forcing traditional organisations to transform their operating and business practices from a linear model to one centered on exponential performance.

Based on the Singularity University's research over a six-year period that included the top 100 fastest growing start-up companies worldwide, researchers identified 10 common external and internal attributes, including a massive transformational purpose across these exponential organisations, summarised in Table 5.

Table 5: Exponential organisations' attributes and characteristics

Attributes	Description
Massive Transformational Purpose	Higher, big aspirational purpose
External attributes (SCALE)	
Staff on demand	Are on-demand staff and on-demand assets utilised?
Community and crowd	Are community and crowd leveraged?
Algorithms	Are algorithms a core part of the organisation?
Leveraged assets	Are business functions externalised?
Engagement	Are its products and services information-based?

Internal attributes (IDEAS)	
Interfaces	Are interfaces created to manage external scalability?
Dashboards	Are key objectives and Lean Metrics used to track performance?
Experimentation	Does the organisation encourage risk-taking and experimentation?
Autonomy	Does the organisation encourage top-down, command and control hierarchies or flat, autonomous, collaborative team structures?
Social	Are social technologies integrated into the organisation?

Source: Singularity University

Based on the attributes in Table 5, researchers created an Exponential Quotient Survey to analyse how exponential an organisation is. Organisations with ExO scores above 55, from a maximum score of 84, were determined to perform exponentially. Table 6 ranks the Fortune 100 companies by their exponential quotient (ExO) score in 2015[92].

Table 6: 2015 Fortune 100 Exponential Quotient ranking

ExO Rank	Company	Year Founded	ExO Score
1	Google	1998	72.9
2	Amazon	1994	66.2
3	Apple	1976	62.6
4	IBM	1911	61
5	Verizon	2000	58.8

6	General Electric	1892	56.6
7	Microsoft	1974	55.9
8	CISCO Systems, Inc.	1984	55.8
9	The Walt Disney Company	1923	54.8
10	Oracle	1977	54
11	The Coca-Cola Company	1892	49.5
12	DirecTV	1990	49
13	McKesson	1833	49
14	United Parcel Service (UPS)	1907	49
15	AT&T	1885	48.8
16	Humana Inc.	1961	48.8
17	State Farm Insurance Cos.	1922	48.4
18	The Allstate Corporation	2008	47.3
19	Lockheed Martin Corporation	1995	47.2
20	Comcast	1963	47
21	American Express Company	1850	46.8
22	Twenty-First Century Fox, Inc.	2013	46.6
23	PepsiCo	1965	46.5
24	Walgreen Co.	1901	46.5
25	Anthem Inc (Wellpoint)	2004	46.4

26	Johnson Controls, Inc.	1885	46
27	Mondelez International, Inc.	1923	45.6
28	Merck & Co., Inc.	1891	45
29	United Continental Holdings, Inc.	1926	45
30	Ford Motor	1903	43.2
31	Lowe's Companies	1946	43
32	United Health Group	1974	43
33	The Home Depot	1978	43
34	Wal-Mart Stores	1962	42.7
35	World Fuel Services Corporation	1984	42.5
36	John Deere Company	1837	42.4
37	Wells Fargo	1852	42.4
38	General Motors	1908	42
39	New York Life Insurance Company	1845	42
40	Supervalu Inc.	1870	42
41	The Goldman Sachs Group, Inc.	1869	41.8
42	Archer Daniels Midland (ADM)	1902	41.8
43	Prudential Financial, Inc.	1875	41.4
44	Target	1962	41.4

45	Sears Holdings Corporation	1893	41.4
46	E.I. du Pont de Nemours and Company (DuPont)	1802	41.3
47	CHS Inc.	1929	41
48	FedEx Corporation	1973	41
49	Kroger	1883	41
50	United Technologies	1934	41
51	Procter & Gamble	1837	40.9
52	Cigna Corporation	1982	40.7
53	Hewlett-Packard	1939	40.7
54	TIAA-CREF	1918	40.7
55	Boeing	1916	40.3
56	CVS Caremark	1892	40
57	Best Buy Co., Inc.	1966	40
58	Intel Corporation	1968	40
59	Liberty Mutual Holding Company Inc.	1912	40
60	Pfizer	1848	39.8
61	Citigroup	1812	39.8
62	Johnson & Johnson	1886	39.3
63	Honeywell International	1906	39.3
64	Ingram Micro Inc.	1979	39.3
65	Massachusetts Mutual Life Insurance Company	1851	39

66	Delta Airlines	1924	39
67	American International Group (AIG)	1919	38.3
68	Express Scripts Holding	1986	38
69	Tyson Foods, Inc.	1935	37.5
70	AmerisourceBergen	2001	37
71	Exxon Mobil	1999	37
72	Nationwide Mutual Insurance Inc.	1926	37
73	Safeway Inc.	1847	36.3
74	Freddie Mac	1970	36.3
75	Sysco Corporation	1969	36
76	MetLife	1868	36
77	Caterpillar	1925	34.5
78	Chevron	1879	34.5
79	ConocoPhillips	2012	34.5
80	General Dynamics Corporation	1952	34.5
81	Cardinal Health	1905	34
82	Dow Chemical	1897	34
83	Fannie Mae	1905	34
84	INTL FCStone Inc.	1905	34
85	Aetna Inc.	1905	33.5
86	Morgan Stanley	1905	33.5
87	Berkshire Hathaway	1839	33.2
88	J.P. Morgan Chase & Co	1904	33

89	Bank of America	1905	32.5
90	Marathon Petroleum	1905	32.3
91	Costco Wholesale	1983	32
92	Philip Morris International Inc.	1847	31.6
93	Hess Corporation	1993	31.3
94	HCA Holdings, Inc.	1968	31
95	Phillips 66	2012	30.7
96	Tesoro Corporation	1968	30
97	Valero Energy	1980	29.8
98	Plains GP Holdings, L.P.	1989	27.5
99	Energy Transfer Equity, L.P.	1995	26.5
100	Enterprise Products Partners L.P.	1968	23

Only eight of the total 100 Fortune organisations are deemed to be performing exponentially, and all of these companies operate in high-tech industries. As shown in Figure 51, the high-tech industry is also the most digitised, with the second highest revenue at risk over the coming years. This analysis illustrates the transformational extent to which traditional organisations must adapt their models to compete with next-generation exponential organisations, particularly those from the telecommunications, professional services, retail and insurance sectors, where the gap of industry digitisation and revenue at risk is much larger than those in advanced stages of digitisation.

Other insights reveal that:

- Of the 15 Fortune 100 organisations founded during the First Industrial Revolution (1700–1870), none are performing exponentially
- Of the 61 Fortune 100 organisations founded during the Second Industrial Revolution (1870–1970), only two are performing exponentially
- Of the 24 Fortune 100 organisations founded during the Third Industrial Revolution, only five are performing exponentially

Unsurprisingly, this analysis clearly highlights the connection and relationship between the age of the organisation and its capacity to adapt. With 40 per cent of Fortune 500 companies predicted to no longer exist within 10 years[93], the majority of the Fortune 100 organisations stuck in the Second Industrial Revolution will find it increasingly difficult to adapt and costlier to transform amidst the disruptive scale and impact of the Fourth Industrial Revolution.

The competitive and indeed existential threat from exponential organisations has become a common narrative on earnings calls. For example, in 2017, Amazon was mentioned nearly 3000 times—more than Facebook, Apple and Microsoft combined[94] (see Figure 56).

Figure 56: Mention of the top five tech companies in earnings call 2008–2015

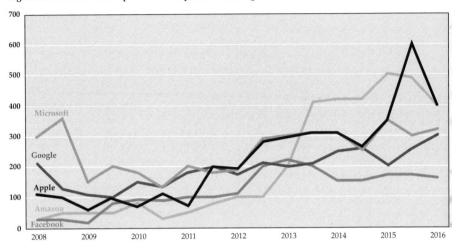

Source: CBInsights
Reproduced by permission

> *When technology platforms work across geographical*
> *boundaries, no one country and no one government*
> *alone can deliver the international norms, rules, and*
> *standards for a global digital world ... The status quo*
> *is increasingly unsustainable as it becomes clear these*
> *platforms are no longer just passive hosts.*
>
> — **British Prime Minister Theresa May**
> *Davos 2018*

With mobile connectivity expected to reach 5.7 billion people by 2020, the addition of one billion connected people fundamentally changes the pace of innovation in a way we have not seen before. As the information enablement of industries, products and services accelerates, there has never been a more important time for traditional, linear-based model organisations to consider their economic and human capital investments to transform to compete in an exponential world. The dematerialisation, demonetisation and democratisation of technologies will put powerful tools in the hands of individuals globally, where in the past they were reserved for major corporations. In their hands, they will dematerialise, disaggregate and disintermediate value chains.

Let's now examine a case study on the digitisation of China's economy, in order to gain insights into what are the critical success factors in that nation transforming itself into a digital powerhouse.

Case study: The digitisation of China's economy

If you want 10,000 customers, you have to build a new warehouse and this and that…. For me, it's two servers.

— Jack Ma
founder and executive chairman, Alibaba Group

In a relatively short time (10 years), China has become a global powerhouse of digital. According to McKinsey[95], China is now in the top three countries in the world for venture capital investment, growing from US$12 billion, or six per cent of total global market share from 2011–13, to attracting US$77 billion, or 19 per cent of total global share over 2014–16. It has now become the world's largest e-commerce market, accounting for 42 per cent of the value of worldwide e-commerce transactions—up from one per cent a decade ago. China has also become a global leader in mobile payments, at 11 times the transaction value of the United States, with more than 460 million users processing US\$9 trillion in 2016[96] (see Figure 57). It's home to one-in-three of the world's 262 unicorns, which represents 43 per cent of the global value of these companies.

While China has a trade deficit in services overall, it now has a trade surplus in digital services of over US\$15 billion per year. The digital capacity and shift towards a consumption rather than investment economic model in the Chinese economy was fueled by a few key factors:

Figure 57: Retail e-commerce transactions, Mobile payment and Unicorns (China, United States, Rest of World 2016))

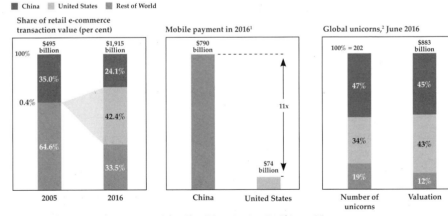

1. Refers to third-party payments conducted through mobile transactions. For China, mobile payments exclude bank or UnionPay credit-card transactions, digital wealth management, and digital finance. For the United States, payments are in-person payments on mobiles between buyers and sellers, and remote payments on mobile devices.

2. Defines as startups valued at \$1 billion or above.

Source: Dealogic; eMarketer; iResearch; PitchBook; TechCrunch's CrunchBase Unicorn Leaderboard; McKinsey Global Institute analysis

1. **Millennial scale**. China has a high concentration of Millennials in its population (31 per cent), but the size of that cohort is enormous—more than 415 million people. That scale is not found in any other region or country. More broadly, other demographic groups within China have developed an unquenchable thirst for connectivity and the internet. In 2016, China had 731 million internet users—again, scale not found in other regions of the world. As illustrated in Figure 9, Chinese Millennials now hold a greater average economic value relative to the average of the total population, underpinning the significant e-commerce and mobile payments growth.

2. **Tech giants.** Baidu, Alibaba and Tencent have developed integrated ecosystems from their platforms, becoming embedded within the lifestyles of Chinese people. While e-commerce is Alibaba's main revenue source, digital media and cloud computing are rapidly growing businesses, with customers in 2017 numbering 900 million. WeChat is the fastest growing Tencent service, with customers in 2017 numbering 980 million. Online games are Tencent's main revenue source.

3. **Government support.** The Chinese government enables digitisation by continuing to be a major investor in, and consumer of, digital technologies; pursuing supportive policies, including promoting competition (by avoiding excessive regulation); and managing labour markets' transition to digital.

According to McKinsey, new applications of the internet could account for up to 22 per cent of China's GDP growth through 2025, translating into 4–14 trillion renminbi. Digitisation is not only seen as benefiting the economy through productivity (estimated to be 22 per cent by 2025), but growth through market expansion.

The Internet of Things (IoT), through increased connectivity and digital content, provides the most significant potential uplift from the current trajectory for consumer electronics, followed by automation in the automotive industry and efficiency gains from digitising financial services. Of interest are projected declines in the real estate and healthcare area from the information enablement and adoption of technologies of those sectors (see Figure 58).

The digitisation of China's economy is expected to boost productivity, create innovation and stimulate growth. The three forces that are predicted to create 10–45 per cent of industry revenue pools through value-chain restructuring by 2030 are: disintermediation (cutting out the middleman), disaggregation (separating processes into components) and dematerialisation (shifting from the physical to digital form) (see Figure 59).

The consumer, retail, freight and logistics sectors stand to benefit most from disintermediation, while automotive and mobility and healthcare stand to benefit the most from disaggregation through value shifts.

Current trajectory

Figure 58: Potential contribution of new applications to China's GDP growth 2013–25 (per cent of sector GDP growth)

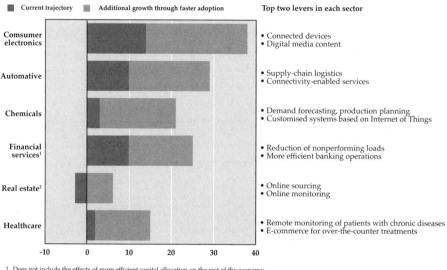

■ Current trajectory   ■ Additional growth through faster adoption

Top two levers in each sector

Comsumer electronics
- Connected devices
- Digital media content

Automative
- Supply-chain logistics
- Connectivity-enabled services

Chemicals
- Demand forecasting, production planning
- Customised systems based on Internet of Things

Financial services[1]
- Reduction of nonperforming loads
- More efficient banking operations

Real estate[2]
- Online sourcing
- Online monitoring

Healthcare
- Remote monitoring of patients with chronic diseases
- E-commerce for over-the-counter treatments

1 Does not include the effects of more efficient capital allocation on the rest of the economy.
2 Potential drop because of internet-related shifts in demand for commercial real estate.

Figure 59: Disintermediation and disaggregation across major Chinese sector (High scenario)

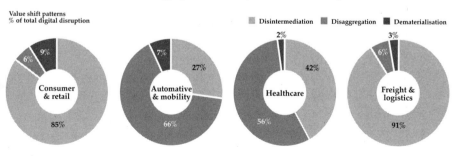

Value shift patterns
% of total digital disruption

■ Disintermediation   ■ Disaggregation   ■ Dematerialisation

Consumer & retail: 9%, 6%, 85%

Automative & mobility: 7%, 27%, 66%

Healthcare: 2%, 42%, 56%

Freight & logistics: 3%, 6%, 91%

China has a widely communicated vision to be a digital world power and is significantly investing in pursuit of that aim. For example, the State Council-led Mass Entrepreneurship and Innovation Program has given rise to 8,000-plus incubators and accelerator programs. The government's guiding fund has invested US$27.4 billion in venture capital and private equity investors. Investments in next-generation 5G wireless networks over the coming years are estimated to be US$180 billion.

Artificial Intelligence: 'Made in China'

In 2017, the State Council released a policy statement of intent indicating that China will be heavily investing to become the world leader in Artificial Intelligence (AI) by 2030, building an industry worth US$150 billion. 'China will become the world's premier Artificial Intelligence innovation center.'[97] China's capabilities in advanced and emerging technologies have lagged behind other major technology areas in Europe and North America, but after a decade of state-supported industrial policy, it will catch up and lead in some areas.

Since I became CEO, 87 per cent of the companies in the Fortune 500 are off the list. What that says is that companies that don't reinvent themselves will be left behind. I also think that's true of people. And I think it's true of countries.

— John T. Chambers
former executive chairman and CEO, CISCO Systems

Chapter summary

- Without digitisation, studies estimated that a third of revenues are at risk of loss or cannibalisation over the next three years.

- Organisations that are digitising and hold significant market share are just as great a threat as new entrants.

- To date, investment in digital has only been proportional to revenues and underinvestment was found to be in industries that stand to gain the most from emerging disruptive technologies.

- Digital leaders and renovators exhibit common characteristics, such as: innovating in their business models in a transformational way; scaling up cutting-edge technologies; investing three times as much; and viewing the world as interconnected ecosystems.

- Digital strategies fail due to their irreconcilable economic, strategic and operational differences between their traditional model and the pace and scale of disruptive transformation.

- Exponential organisations leverage multiplication effects, information enablement, acceleration and exponential technologies to outperform peers and competitors by 10 times.

- Only eight of the Fortune 100 are deemed to be performing exponentially, illustrating the transformational extent to which traditional organisations have to adapt their models and compete against next-generation exponential organisations.

- As technology platforms transcend the traditional trading boundaries, governments will increasingly rely on cross-border policy alignment.

- The digitisation of China's economy was fueled by a few interrelated factors: Millennial population scale, tech giants and government support. Disintermediation, dematerialisation and disaggregation are the major forces in value-chain restructuring.

Chapter Nine

DATA, ANALYTICS AND ARTIFICIAL INTELLIGENCE

The 21st century's energy

In God we trust — All others bring data

—W. Edwards Deming
statistician

Hollywood has long filled our imaginations with the science fiction possibilities of Artificial Intelligence with films such as *Star Wars, Blade Runner, I, Robot* and *The Matrix,* just to name a few. My favourite is *The Terminator,* an American film directed by James Cameron. This was Arnold Schwarzenegger's 1984 defining role as the cyborg sent back in time. The Cyberdyne Systems T-800 Model 101 had living tissue over a metal endoskeleton designed for combat and infiltration.

The movie's central notion of a future retrospective capability informs our inquisition of the possibility of predicting something that is yet to occur. Interestingly, it was reported that Schwarzenegger tried to change the now famous line 'I'll be back' due to his accent and pronunciation. His reasoning was that the terminator would not speak in contractions. As we know, Cameron had the foresight in 1984 to know that Artificial Intelligence (AI) could one day problem-solve linguistic- and contraction-related challenges. Our technological advancements have today put us on an exponential development pathway to the wonders AI can offer us in the future—however, we are far from getting the basics of data right.

The efficiency and effectiveness of how organisations use data is a major source of competitive advantage. Equally, our digital lives, real-time expectations and personalised experiences have been shaped on a well-orchestrated symphony of data. In this chapter we will explore these dimensions to understand why some organisations have become analytical competitors and are set to capitalise on the Fourth Industrial Revolution, and why others haven't.

Data is the digital lifeblood for how we live our lives, and run our businesses, our economies and even our governments. The scale of data has simply surpassed the ability of human cognition. Not only are we incapable of processing the data, we are no longer capable of understanding its characteristics.

Data is the source of our digital existence. But unlike natural resources, the way we prospect for it, mine it, capture and develop it, store it, secure it, value-add to it, distribute it and ultimately consume it, means there is an infinite supply of this valuable resource—and we can somehow afford inefficiency and ineffectiveness because of its abundance. In fact, it is this abundance that creates a fundamental problem: the ability to identify and exploit the data that matters in a seemingly inexhaustible flood. Data also has some fundamentally different properties: unlike physical assets, the value of data increases through sharing and reuse.

We also expect it will fuel the infinite supply of devices by which the world will be connected. While data is the competitive currency of organisations in this digital age, few treat it as such.

The other dimension that we need to consider is trust. As discussed in Chapter Five, data breaches will continue to erode trust in institutions that are the custodians of their customers, employees and investors' personal information. This is particularly true for Millennials, where banks are the most trusted with their personal information.

We define analytics as the use of data, sophisticated quantitative and statistical analysis, explanatory and predictive modelling and fact-based management to drive decision-making. In this chapter, we will explore how to use this to out-think competitors. I'll draw upon the wonderful research by Davenport and Harris in the book *Competing on Analytics — The New Science of Winning*[98]. Their comprehensive research has mapped the DNA of an 'analytical competitor' and how they use analytics as their secret weapon for competitive advantage.

Artificial Intelligence and machine learning are two of the hottest topics at the moment and tend to be described as though they are the same thing. They're not. We define Artificial Intelligence as computer systems (including robots) capable of performing tasks normally associated with human intelligence, such as visual perception, speech recognition or decision-making. The term is associated with the intellectual process characteristics of humans such as the ability to reason, discover meaning, generalise or learn from past experience. Machine learning, on the other hand, is where algorithms create models without human involvement. Traditional machine learning does need human involvement to identify the interesting features in the data used to build a model. Deep learning no longer relies on humans to identify the interesting features in data.

Data

Data has indeed evolved exponentially, doubling virtually every 12 months. According to IDC forecasts[99], by 2025 the global data sphere (defined as the sum of all data created, captured, and replicated on our planet in any given year) is set to reach 163 zettabytes (ten times the 16.1ZB generated in 2016). They describe five key data trends that are expected to change our world.

1. *Data evolves to become life-critical.* Evolving from siloed, fragmented, underutilised data to become essential to society and our lives. They estimate that by 2025, 20 per cent of data will be critical to our daily lives, with 10 per cent being hypercritical (see Figure 60).
2. *Embedded systems and the Internet of Things (IoT).* As our lives, businesses, appliances, sensors, etc., become interconnected into ecosystems, they will generate exponential amounts of

Figure 60: Data critically over time

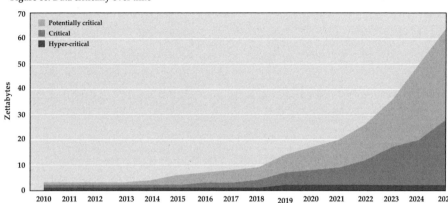

Data type	CAGR 2015–2015
All Data. Includes all data in the global datasphere.	30%
Potentially critical. Data that may be necessary to the continued, convenient operation of users' daily lives.	37%
Critical. Data known to be necessary for the expected continuity of users' daily lives.	39%
Hypercritical. Data with direct and immediate impact on the health and well being of users. (Examples include commercial air travel, medical applications, control systems, and telemetry. The category is heavy in metadata and data from embedded systems.	54%

Source: IDCs's Data Age 2025 study, sponsored by Seagate, April 2017
Reprinted by permission

data. Experts predict that by 2025, an average person will interact with connected devices around 4,800 times per day (one interaction every 18 seconds). See Figure 61.

3. *Mobile and real-time data.* The global ubiquity of mobile devices equips us to access data, whether explicitly or implicitly, through our consumption of data-driven services, whenever and wherever we need it. By 2025, it is predicted that more than 25 per cent of data created will be real-time, and data originated from IoT will represent 95 per cent of this (see Figure 62).

4. *Cognitive systems that change the landscape.* Emerging technologies such as machine learning, natural language

Figure 61: Interactions per connected person per day

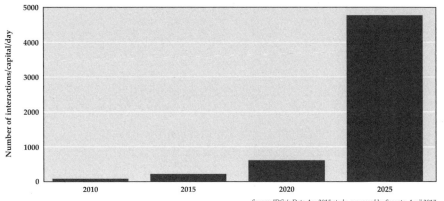

Source: IDCs's Data Age 2015 study, sponsored by Seagate, April 2017
Reprinted by permission

Figure 62: Mobile data

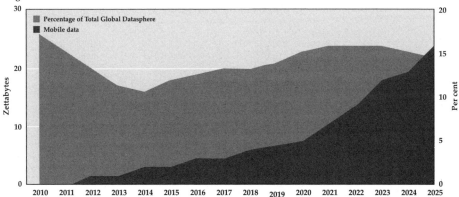

Source: IDCs's Data Age 2025 study, sponsored by Seagate, April 2017
Reprinted by permission

Figure 63: Data tagging

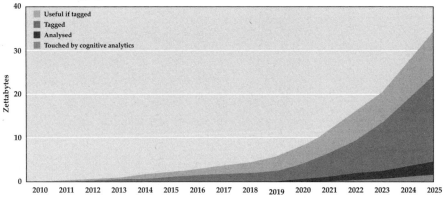

Source: IDCs's Data Age 2025 study, sponsored by Seagate, April 2017
Reprinted by permission

processing and Artificial Intelligence (collectively referred to as cognitive systems) convert data analysis into intelligence. Cognitive automation replicates human actions and judgements at tremendous speed, scale, quality and lower cost. By 2025, the amount of analysed data will grow by a factor of 50 to 5.2ZB, and the amount of analysed data exposed to cognitive systems will grow by a factor of 100 to 1.4ZB (see Figure 63).

5. *Data security.* The volume, velocity, variety, value, validity, veracity and volatility (V-Model) of data creates exposures as its value to criminals increases exponentially. It is predicted that by 2025, 90 per cent of all data will require some form of security, but less than half will be secured (see Figure 64).

What these trends illustrate is that this resource will become even more mission critical, more broadly captured, available in

Figure 64: Status of data security

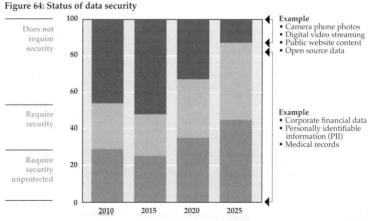

Source: IDCs's Data Age 2025 study, sponsored by Seagate, April 2017
Reprinted by permission

real-time, processed intelligently and unsecured. If we were to consider any other organisational resource in the same way, it would be treated as an asset. We would also measure that asset's utilisation, as it would become a vital economic performance indicator. In so doing, we need to shift our thinking away from considering data in an abundant manner—where our aim is to squirrel it away during winter to feast on it during the summer—to treating data as organisational intelligence, and optimising the use of this asset.

Recognising the impact that data has on the competitiveness of industries and markets, innovation and the significant benefits to consumers associated with greater levels of control of their data, governments in the United Kingdom, Israel, Singapore and Australia are moving to regulate open data access regimes. While the financial services industry has been a lead target industry for open data reforms, the telecommunications and energy industries are also in policy makers' line of sight.

Analytics

Against this statistical backdrop, big data has become not only a strategic but also an existential imperative. So why compete on analytics? The Third Industrial Revolution not only eroded many of the traditional sources of competitive advantage, but gave rise to the information enablement of many products and services delivered through platforms that changed the economic physics of industries—referred to more commonly as disruption. New exponential models emerged that were platform-based, capital-light and data-intensive.

Analytics has become the number one strategic and investment priority for many organisations[100], including leveraging these analytics investments to experiment and explore the global data sphere of unstructured data (raw unanalysed data), prospecting for insights that structured data sets may not reveal.

We define an analytical competitor as an organisation that uses analytics extensively and systematically to out-think and out-execute the competition. Research by Davenport and Harris of 371 medium-to-large organisations found that the most analytically sophisticated and successful organisations exhibited four common characteristics:

1. Analytics supported a strategic, distinctive capability
2. The approach to and management of analytics was enterprise-wide
3. Senior management was committed to the use of analytics
4. The company made a strategic bet on analytics-based competition

What they found was that analytical competitors achieved superior performance. A study by Accenture and Massachusetts Institute of Technology (MIT) found that 92 per cent of high-performing organisations reported achieving significant ROI from analytics, versus only 24 per cent of low performers. They found that despite organisations selecting the best technologies, their capacity for change limited their chances of success with analytics[101]. The main factors were:

- Lack of analytics vision and missing the right sponsorship
- Inability to shift culture
- Politics and an inability to change
- Too little stakeholder engagement

Critically, Davenport and Harris's research found that only five per cent of organisations were analytical competitors, illustrating the significant data and analytics transformational effort required by traditional organisations. Let's refer back to the relationship between analytical competitors and exponential performance, where just eight per cent of the Fortune 100 were deemed to be performing exponentially. What we know is one of the underlying characteristics of exponential organisations is that they leverage data, analytics and algorithms to achieve superior performance.

So how do organisations become analytical competitors? Researchers also identified five stages of maturity that organisations progress through as part of their data analytics transformations (see Table 7).

Table 7: Stages of analytical competitiveness maturity

Stage	Capability distinctiveness	Objective
1 Analytically Impaired	Negligible, 'flying blind'	Get accurate data to improve operations
2 Localised Analytics	Local and opportunistic—may not be supporting company's distinctive capabilities	Use analytics to improve one or more functional activities
3 Analytical Aspirant	Begin efforts for more integrated data and analytics	Use analytics to improve a distinctive capability
4 Analytical Company	Enterprise-wide perspective, able to use analytics for point advantage, know what to do to get to next level, but not quite there	Build broad analytic capability—analytics for differentiation
5 Analytical Competitor	Enterprise-wide big results, sustainable advantage	Analytical master— fully competing on analytics

Source: Davenport & Harris

Technology in the Third Industrial Revolution dematerialised, disintermediated and disaggregated the competitive advantage of many organisations and the products and services they offered. Globalisation further eroded any geographical or protective regulatory advantages that industries, organisations and governments relied upon. Intelligence and its execution have become the new frontiers resetting competitive landscapes and distinguishing the winners from the losers. Data and analytics are the capabilities that explain superior market and economic performance.

Predictive analytics unlocks the power of data—the world's greatest booming unnatural resource. We define predictive analytics as the practice of extracting information from existing data sets in order to determine patterns and predict the future. This should not be confused with descriptive analytics, which is used to interpret historical data and what may have occurred. Nor should it be confused with prescriptive analytics, which is the area of business analytics dedicated to finding the best course of action. The type of analytics used in an organisation shouldn't be thought of as an either/or choice. They all play an important role in the analytical capability of an organisation.

Technology now learns from data and experience is now able to predict behaviour. We live in a predictive society obsessed by a desire to know.

We have all been 'predicted' in some aspect of our life—whether its companies presenting ads to us, insurers pricing risk, government checking entitlements (or tax compliance), law enforcement or hospitals for illnesses. But prediction seems to defy a law of nature: you cannot see the future, because it isn't here yet! With apologies to Terminator fans, 'I'll be back' remains an imagined scenario for the time being. So, we develop and build technologies that learn from experience, to place accurate odds on what's coming. 'I'll be back', but with a zero per cent level of confidence.

Artificial Intelligence

Our contemporary application of the concept of Artificial Intelligence has advanced with our knowledge of how our brain works. Its earlier use focused on complex calculations by reproducing capabilities such as arithmetic and memory. Today it focuses on emulating human decision-making processes and carrying out complex human tasks.

Artificial Intelligence has found its place due to an exponential price/performance cost reduction and increase in computer power and storage. The tsunami of data has also driven a focus on AI as a coping mechanism. The past decade has seen unprecedented algorithmic advancements—many associated with machine learning. The ability to apply machine learning to vast data sets using algorithms to detect patterns and trends, and then learn how to predict and recommend, has been a significant breakthrough. Deep learning is a subset of machine learning but can process a broader range of data sets. Deep learning has interconnected layers of algorithm-based calculators called neurons, which form a neural network by feeding data into one another.

Artificial Intelligence has been widely embraced in consumer markets. Language-based virtual assistants such as Google Assistant, Microsoft Cortana, and Apple's Siri are now widely used through our smartphones, smart vehicles and in our smart homes. Commercial applications are also rapidly emerging, for example, interpreting video feeds from drones carrying out visual inspections and even in rescue situations. In Australia, lifeguards used a drone to save two people from drowning at Lennox Head in New South Wales[102]. Not only was the drone used to locate the swimmers that were in trouble, but it was also able to drop lifesaving floatation equipment to them until rescuers arrived—all within 70 seconds from the time the drone was launched.

Technology companies are now in a race, and as we saw with the case study on the digitisation of the Chinese economy, the race is on among nations. Some of the leading players include IBM with its Watson technology and Google with its DeepMind and AlphaGo. Technology companies have invested billions of dollars to develop AI capability that are cloud-enabled as platforms, allowing them to scale and be deployed worldwide. These technology companies aren't the only ones to exploit their service sets—they expose them through their cloud platforms for other organisations that want to consume machine learning Artificial Intelligence models, providing on-demand such as voice, vision, language and recognition services.

What are the benefits of Artificial Intelligence?

According to PwC[103], AI could drive GDP gains of US$15.7 trillion with productivity and personalisation improvements. It claims global GDP could be 14 per cent higher in 2030 as a result of Artificial Intelligence, of which productivity improvements could account for about half. PwC also reports that the greatest economic gains from AI will be in China (26 per cent growth in GDP by 2030) and in North America (14.5 per cent growth)—the equivalent of US$10.7 trillion. It's pretty obvious why these countries are in an Artificial Intelligence race.

At an industry level, its analysis reveals those that stand to benefit most (score of 5) and the least (score of 1) (see Table 8).

Table 8: Industry benefits from Artificial Intelligence

Industry	Benefit Significance from Artificial Intelligence
Healthcare (providers, health services, pharmaceutical, life sciences, insurance, consumer health)	3.7
Automotive (after market and repair, components suppliers, personal mobility, OEM, financing)	3.7
Financial Services (asset wealth management, banking and capital, insurance)	3.3
Transportation & Logistics	3.2
Technology, Communication & Entertainment	3.1
Retail (consumer products)	3.0
Energy (oil and gas, power, utilities)	2.2
Manufacturing (industrial, products, raw materials)	2.2

Source: PWC

The eruption of Artificial Intelligence means that within the next five years we are likely to see AI competitors emerge across many sectors. To traditional organisations struggling to transform their data and analytics environments, analytical competitors will be able to attack their business models in ways and at scales that traditional organisations will struggle to detect and respond to. The giant leap is shifting our thinking away from this resource and its abundance, to it becoming the primary organisational intelligence.

At an industry level, use cases for both advanced analytics and AI applications are emerging rapidly. While advanced analytics has much greater value creation potential relative to AI, the greatest potential value from these use cases are evenly split between marketing and sales and supply-chain management and manufacturing (see Figure 65)[104].

This highlights the potential of AI to improve business model performance on both income generation and operational efficiency. However, at a functional level, risk management and compliance and service operations are most likely to create greater value through the use of advanced analytics and AI, relative to product development, strategy and corporate finance, and human resource management.

I began this chapter with the famous quote 'In God we trust—All others bring data', attributed to W. Edwards Deming, reputed as the father of modern quality management. Deming was reportedly heavily involved in the economic reconstruction of

Figure 65: Value creation by function (US$ trillion)

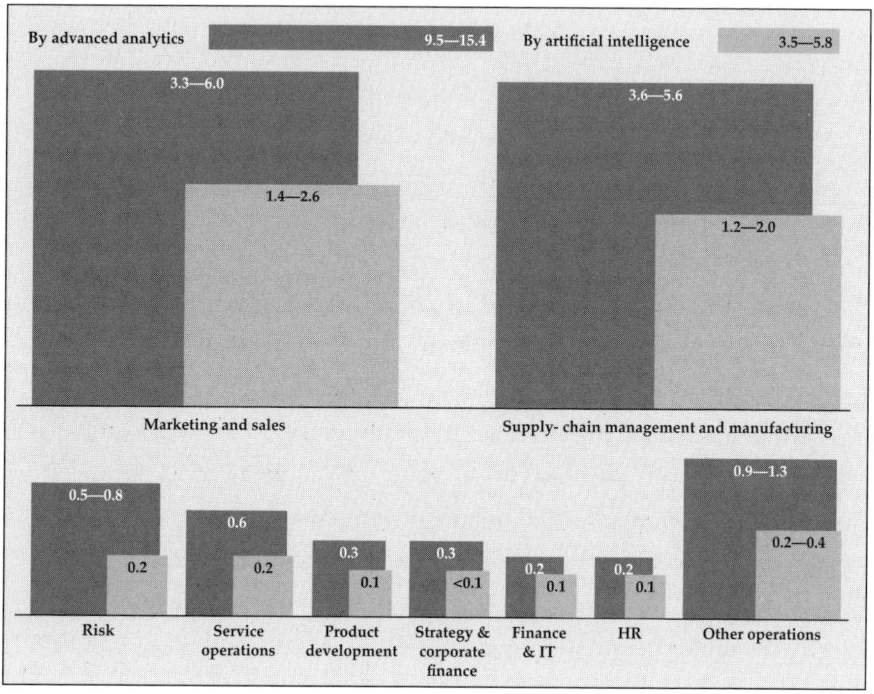

Source: Exhibit from "Notes from the AI frontier: Applications and value of deep learning", April 2018, McKinsey Global Institute, www.mckinsey.com. © 2018 McKinsey & Company. All rights reserved. Reprinted by permission.

Japan after World War II. From that period of time through to the 1980s, Japanese history was characterised by its rise in scaled manufacturing and total quality management practices. There has never been a more important time to consider the significance of Deming's principle, i.e., that data measurement and analysis are critical to superior performance in every aspect of business, as there is today.

However, while Deming's philosophy has been known and respected for a while, a significant gap has emerged between the trust leaders feel in the criticality of data and analytics to their performance, and the confidence they have in their own organisation's data and analytics capabilities. According to a commissioned study of 2,200 global information technology and business decision-makers by Forrester Consulting on behalf of KPMG International,[105] just 35 per cent reported having a high level of trust in their own organisation's analytics, and six per cent reported an active distrust and reluctance to use their organisation's data. This was despite the fact that 92 per cent were concerned about the impact of analytics on their organisation's corporate reputation.

At a country level, the study found a wide range of confidence levels. For example, India held the highest level of trust in data and analytics at 65 per cent, and the United Kingdom the lowest at just 21 per cent. When it came to active distrust or reluctance to use their organisation's data, the United Kingdom results were the highest at 15 per cent, and Brazil and China the lowest at 2 per cent.

We've seen in this chapter that not only is data growth predicted to increase exponentially, but that by 2025, a third of that data is expected to become critical to our daily lives. Importantly, we've seen that with the Internet of Things (IoT), 90 per cent of this data will require some form of security, but less than half is predicted to be secured. Without the strategic priority of organisations to close this gap, this will exponentially impact trust in an AI- and data-driven world. The benefits anticipated through AI will go unrealised at a national, organisational and personal level.

Artificial Intelligence (AI) is the most important thing humanity has ever worked on. I think of it as something more profound than electricity or fire.

— **Sundar Pichai**
CEO Google

Chapter summary

- Data has evolved to become critical, embedded, real-time and mobile.

- Emerging cognitive systems convert data analytics into intelligence, replicating human actions and judgment at speed, scale and quality at lower cost.

- The speed at which it has developed has outpaced security, which creates exposures.

- Analytical competitors are outperforming their peers in productivity and profitability, but are far and few, reflecting the significant transformation required by traditional organisations.

- The eruption of Artificial Intelligence means that within the next five years we are likely to see AI competitors emerge across many sectors.

- AI could drive GDP gains of US$15.7 trillion (14 per cent) with productivity and personalisation improvements.

- While advanced analytics offers much greater value-creation potential relative to AI, both are predicted to evenly generate value from marketing and sales and supply chain and manufacturing use cases.

- Unlocking the potential of AI, however, will require reconciling the gap between confidence in an organisation's data and analytics, with those concerns about its impact on corporate reputation.

- In the short term, not closing that gap will increase the risk of further eroding trust in organisations.

Chapter Ten

THE FOURTH INDUSTRIAL REVOLUTION

Coming, ready or not

> *The greatest danger in times of turbulence is not the*
> *turbulence — it is to act with yesterday's logic.*

— Peter Drucker
management consultant, educator and author

If nations and organisations aren't yet fully capitalising on the Third Industrial Revolution, how ready are they for the fourth? Not very, according to Deloitte Global and Forbes Insights, which asked that question of 1,600 C-level executives in business and government across 19 countries. Only 14 per cent reported they were ready in four key areas: social impact, strategy, talent and technology[106].

The study also found that:

- The private sector was considered to have the most influence on how the Fourth Industrial Revolution shapes society (public business organisations 74 per cent; private business organisations 67 per cent).

- Despite this, executives were not confident in the level of influence their own organisations would have over societal factors (agent of change 24 per cent; serving underserved markets/accessibility/affordability 19 per cent).
- Over the next five years, executives reported that changing regulation and emergence of new delivery models would have the greatest impact on their organisations (changing regulation 41 per cent; new delivery models 40 per cent; economic trade landscape 32 per cent).
- While executives recognise the need to invest in technology to drive new business models, making the business case inhibits investment due to lack of strategic alignment and focus on the short term (lack of alignment 43 per cent; lack of collaboration with partners 38 per cent; short-termism 37 per cent).
- Relative to all organisations surveyed, high-growth organisations more often see themselves as 'architects of society' as well as business leaders.

The results reveal some interesting contradictions. On the one hand, executives believe overwhelmingly (87 per cent) that the private sector will have the most influence in how this revolution will shape society; yet the same optimism was not reflected in their own organisation (24 per cent). At an individual level, only a third are confident of acting as stewards in their organisations, and only 14 per cent are highly confident their organisations are ready to benefit from this revolution.

Despite recognising that the emergence of new businesses and delivery models would pose the greatest threats, executives continue to rely on strategies that prioritise traditional business operations and models. When it comes to workforces, 86 per cent of executives reported that they are doing everything possible to create a better workforce for this revolution, but less than a quarter are highly confident they have the right workforce composition and skills for it.

Using yesterday's logic to prepare your leaders, organisations or policies will not set leaders on the right trajectory for the Fourth Industrial Revolution. We need new thinking, as history has no precedent for what's to come. While this revolution builds on the digital revolution, it will be unlike all others in terms of its speed, impact and scale. It will be a cyber-physical social system, characterised by new technologies that merge the physical, digital and biological worlds, and is predicted to impact all disciplines, economies and industries globally.

This revolution is expected to also witness the emergence of breakthrough technologies in the areas of Artificial Intelligence, robotics, the IoT, autonomous vehicles, blockchain, 3D printing, quantum computing and nanotechnology.

To inform this chapter, I'll draw upon the cutting-edge research, development and leadership of Klaus Schwab and Nicholas David of the World Economic Forum, as outlined in their book, *Shaping the Fourth Industrial Revolution*[107].

What makes this industrial revolution different from others?
According to the World Economic Forum, there are three reasons why this is not just an extension of the Third Industrial Revolution, but is distinct. Let's reflect on these.

1. **Exponential versus linear time.** We explored in Chapter Eight how platform-based, data-intensive and capital-light models exhibited four distinct characteristics. First, the *multiplication effect,* where price/performance of computation doubles about every 18 months. Second, *information enablement,* where once an industry, product or technology becomes information-enabled, its price/performance doubles approximately every year. Third, *acceleration*—once doubling begins, it doesn't stop. And last, *exponential technologies,* i.e., information-enabling technologies. I also highlighted in earlier chapters how the Millennials' population size, economic power, workplace influence and technological influence has altered both demand and supply curves that now behave more exponentially.

2. **Capacity augmentation.** In Chapter Eight, I analysed disruption across industries and organisations, noting that leaders and organisations are yet to capitalise on the full potential of the technologies delivered by the Third Industrial Revolution, leaving them under-prepared for the augmentation of emerging technologies. In Chapters Five, Six and Seven I explored the impact of the trust crisis and Millennials' changing workplace preferences and longevity on the future demand and supply of skills, production and the role of businesses in society.

3. **Systems impact.** We explored in Chapter Eight the value-chain restructuring effect of these disruptions through disintermediation, dematerialisation and disaggregation, and how the emergence of new business models is transforming production, consumption and fulfilment. We looked at the digitisation of China's economy as a case study of how a nation, its industries, and investment policies and programs support its transformation.

In the past 10 years, price/performance has seen the costs of processing power, bandwidth, and cloud infrastructure decline exponentially. This is now powering a new generation of emerging technologies that are fusing the digital, physical and biological worlds. Let's examine each one in turn.

A digital world

As already discussed, we are now living in a mobile media-first world where by 2020, global penetration of smartphones will reach 60 per cent of the world's population. Cities are predicted to be home to 86 per cent of global populations by 2050 and these cities will become smarter as they become increasingly digitally connected. The Internet of Things (IoT) describes the convergence of connected technologies that by 2025 is predicted to connect 20 billion devices—three for every person interacting, some 4,800 times per day through connected devices. Other analysts predict that sensors could number in the trillions. Importantly, these will become inter-connected ecosystems. IoT will be the one of the critical enablers of the 21st century's energy data.

It is predicted that by 2025, 20 per cent of data will be critical to our daily lives and 10 per cent hypercritical. It is also predicted that 25 per cent of that data will be in real-time, and 95 per cent originating from the IoT. Cognitive systems (machine learning, natural language processing and Artificial Intelligence) convert data analysis into intelligence that automates and replicates human actions and judgement at high speed, mass scale, better-than-human quality and lower cost. That is why the IoT is so important. But with exponential increases in our connections comes an exponential threat to our cyber security. Ninety per cent of the data created by 2025 will require some form of security, yet predictions are that only half will be secured.

Connectivity will continue to fundamentally change the way we manage our lives, businesses, industries and governments. Supply chains will become more efficient, assets better utilised, and healthcare better managed through monitoring systems, transactions processed in 'trusted' real-time, crime prevented, etc. The impact of these technology-enabled platforms will be profound, giving rise to completely new ways of consuming goods and services, referred to as the *on-demand economy*. In Chapter Eight, we looked at examples of platform-based, data-intensive, capital-light exponential models such as Uber and Alibaba. Importantly, what I outlined was that these models reach a new *economic physics* where the marginal cost of supply or demand becomes virtually zero. The on-demand economy has lowered barriers, globalising disruption that in 2017 saw US$164 billion of venture capital flow into individuals and businesses. These platforms have decoupled production and scale from demand and supply of scarce resources, bringing into question 'ownership versus access'.

Let's take a look at some of the key technological developments.

Quantum computing

Quantum computers are built on the principles of quantum mechanics and exploit complex laws of nature that are always present but hidden from view. Whereas computing requires data to be encoded into binary digits (bits either 0 or 1), quantum computers employ quantum bits (qubits), which operate according to two key principles of physics: superposition and entanglement. Superposition means that each qubit can represent both a 1 and a 0 at the same time. Entanglement means that qubits in a superposition can be correlated with each other. Areas and industries that could be revolutionised by quantum computing include[108]:

- *Medicine and materials*—untangling the complexity of molecular and chemical interactions, leading to the discovery of new medicines and materials.
- *Supply chain and logistics*—discovering the ideal solution for ultra-efficient logistics and global supply chains.
- *Financial services*—discovering new ways to model financial data and isolating key global risk factors in financial markets.
- *Artificial Intelligence*—making aspects of AI such as machine learning more powerful when data sets are very large.

There still are many physical and engineering aspects of quantum computing that remain unsolved. One of the most significant is trust and security. Quantum computing has the capacity to undermine many current cryptographic technologies used in our computing environment. We would need to find new forms of quantum-resistant cryptography.

Blockchain and distributed ledger technologies

Distributed ledgers use many independent computers (nodes) to record, share and synchronise transactions in their digital ledgers. In contrast, traditional ledger technologies maintain records in a centralised, trusted ledger. Blockchain is one type of distributed ledger.

Distributed ledger technology is transformative in so far as it is expected to be more efficient, resilient and reliable relative to centralised systems. It can restructure value chains by disintermediating (removing intermediaries), disaggregating (separating processes into components) and dematerialising (shifting from physical to digital form). Cross-industry applications are emerging in financial services, government, manufacturing, and settlements systems. Given the global networks this new disruptive technology enables, industries, governments and the private sector will need to resolve many legal, regulatory, technological and integrity issues.

Blockchain and distributed ledgers use cryptography and peer-to-peer transfers to create an immutable digital record (asset, money, securities, land titles, smart contracts, etc.) without the requirement of a central authority. Consensus reportedly provides confidence that information stored and shared between participants is both accurate and transparent. This allows verification and immutability, without requiring a trusted third party to hold record of the details. The technology is also programmable software, which means that transactions can be verified without human involvement, offering the potential for smart contracts. The distributed trust aspects of the technology can benefit supply chains through creating immutable unique identity and verifiable records for chain of custody.

There are four topologies of this technology. First, consortium-based blockchains, where a pre-selected group controls the consensus. Second, private blockchains that are controlled by a single participant that determines who can view, write and participate in the consensus. Third, public blockchains, where anyone can view, write and participate in the consensus. Last, semi-private blockchains, again, run by a single participant; however, they grant access to others who meet a specified criterion. Just some of the use cases that this technology is being developed for include:

- *Crypto-currencies*—one of the best-known applications, Bitcoin, described as a decentralised virtual currency.
- *Supply chain and logistics*—self-executing contracts that transfer risk, value and insurance, verifying the transaction or any associated claims with pre and post authorisations and instructions.

- *Currency exchange and remittance*—perhaps the most advanced use cases, with financial institutions focused on cross-border payments. Pioneers include Ripple.
- *Provenance and chain of custody*—time stamping features in agriculture (e.g. from paddock to plate).
- *Record management*—improve medical record management to store health care data and manage medical records.
- *Decentralised markets*—enabling people anywhere to trade with one another without requiring an institution.

McKinsey research[109] identified 60 nascent use cases of the technology across multiple industries. However, they found that financial services were the primary focus in the areas of payments and capital markets, where significant value creation potential was estimated to range between US$70–85 billion. They also predicted that blockchain technology would reach its full potential by 2023.

What distinguishes this technology's development is the collaboration requirement. Financial services institutions have been earlier pioneers, demonstrating their capacity to work through the standards, legal, regulatory, commercial and other issues to create ecosystems for the use of this technology. There are still significant challenges, such as legal ambiguities, technology infrastructure and standards that can only be resolved through industry collaborative transformation.

The Internet of Things (IoT)

The IoT is described as a system of interconnected and interrelated physical devices, computers, systems, software, appliances, embedded electronics, and sensors that gather and process data according to specified requirements.

By 2025, it is predicted that some 20 billion devices will be connected and that the global IoT market will grow from US$157 billion in 2016 to US$457 billion by 2020[110]. Analysts predict that the global market share will be dominated by three sectors: smart cities (26 per cent), industrial IoT (24 per cent) and connected health (20 per cent). Other sectors include: smart homes (14 per cent), connected cars (seven per cent), smart utilities (four per cent) and wearables (three per cent)[111]. Expectations are high for IoT's potential impact on the global economy, estimated by the World Economic Forum and Accenture to be US$14 trillion by 2030[112].

According to McKinsey[113], by 2025 the IoT will have the potential economic impact of US$3.9–11.1 trillion (see Figure 66). Based on its analysis, we can see that it is industrial use in factories that potentially will gain the greatest impact at both the low estimate and high estimate (US$1.2–3.7 trillion), followed by cities (US$ 930 billion to US$1.7 trillion).

Underpinning this value creation are three capability areas:

- *Data.* Sensors, devices and other equipment can generate contextual data based on events, performance and status that enables factories to perform optimally, be maintained predictively and so avoiding unproductive down time, and improving just-in-time logistics. In cities, public safety can

Figure 66: Potential economic impact of IoT in 2015, including consumer surplus, is US\$ trillion to US\$11.1 trillion

		Size in 2025[1] $billion, adjusted to 2015 dollars Total = $3.9 trillion–11.1 trillion	■ Low estimate ■ High estimate **Major application**
	Human	170–1,590	Monitoring and managing illness, improving wellness
	Home	200–150	Energy ,management, safety and security, chore automation, usage-based design of appliances
	Retail environments	410–1,160	Automated check, layout organisation, smart CRM, in-store personalised promotions, inventory shrinkage prevention
	Offices	70–150	Organisational redesign and worker monitoring, augmented reality training, energy monitoring, building security
	Factories	1,210–3,700	Operations optimisation, predictive maintenance, inventory optimisation, health and safety
	Worksites	160–930	Operations optimisation, equipment maintenance, health and safety, IoT-enabled R&D
	Vehicles	210–740	Condition-based maintenance, reduced insurance
	Cities	930–1,660	Public safety and health, traffic control, resource management
	Outside	560–850	Logistics routing, autonomous cars and trucks, navigation

1. Includes sized applications only
NOTE. Numbers may not sum due to rounding

be improved, and transport optimised—which will reduce the social, economic and environmental impact of congestion.

- *System orchestration,* where devices connected to the same networks can co-ordinate data and instructions among themselves to improve efficiency and effectiveness.

- *Interactive networked devices* coupled with Artificial Intelligence allow for optimisation, such as automation of energy management and retail services.

Improving the operational efficiency of industries and their supply and value chains creates an opportunity for the second wave of value through extension into customer-facing activities, ultimately resulting in improved customer experiences. However, as mentioned in Chapter Nine, for IoT to deliver its full potential, outstanding concerns around the security shortcomings of devices, cultural acceptance, privacy concerns and norms and regulations on how IoT-generated data can be accessed and exploited will be critical.

Physical world

The main manifestations of developments to date are in autonomous vehicles, 3D printing, advanced robotics and new materials. Let's examine each of these.

Artificial Intelligence and robotics

The combination of AI and robotics gained prominence with a significant representation at the 2018 Consumer Electronics Show and, of course, the 2018 Winter Olympic Games. AI is one of the most exciting fields in robotics and a significant interdisciplinary area of engineering research, which includes mechanical construction, electrical components and computer programming and human interface technologies.

Breakthroughs in material science, locomotion and sensory technologies have improved the orchestration of networked machines and their ability to move in different environments. Cognition enables them to be choreographed, as we saw with the use of drones in a fly-over in the opening ceremony of the 2018

Winter Games. Artificial Intelligence allows machines to perform complex navigation and interactivity in an autonomous way.

The combination of Artificial Intelligence and robotics raises many complex issues in areas such as responsibility and accountability. For example, unintended programmatic bias, data regulation and mechanisms for resolving conflict between autonomous and non-autonomous actors in the systems.

The automotive industry has been one of the largest users of automated robots in assembly lines. But as we saw in Chapter Six, all industries will be impacted by automation over the coming years, and many parts of economies will be impacted in terms of improved productivity, elimination of labour-based jobs and the creation of new jobs and services. Manufacturing, transport and logistics industries are likely to be the sectors that will continue investing to further improve production, assembly and distribution. But other sectors are rapidly adopting these technologies, such as:

- *Manufacturing*—assembly lines, e.g., automotive industry
- *Mining*—extracting and processing minerals from the ground
- *Healthcare*—surgical procedures
- *Agriculture*—weed and pesticide management
- *Entertainment*—science fiction motion pictures

Countries such as China, India, Germany and the US, who have significant manufacturing sectors, will likely be the major early investors and due to the large-scale impact on labour markets, will face significant challenges to current government policy settings. However, accelerated adoption of Artificial Intelligence and information process automation will see the impact broadening out across many other sectors and to less manufacturing-centered economies.

Autonomous vehicles

Autonomous vehicles were one of the main showpieces at the 2018 Consumer Electronics Show in the US, which had automation as a key theme. Some of the major developments showcased were:

- Toyota, with its e-Palette concept shuttle vehicle, which they describe as a fully automated, next-generation, battery-powered electronic vehicle, designed to be scalable and customizable for a range of 'mobility-as-a-service' businesses.
- Lyft (a ridesharing company) provided attendees with driverless rides in 20 locations around Las Vegas.
- TuSimple, a Chinese company founded in 2015, showcased its autonomous truck technology.
- Self-flying cab / drones designed to break the traffic gridlock chocking many cities.

Rather than being stand-alone devices, autonomous vehicles are now evolving into synchronised and even self-organising groups, as demonstrated in the opening ceremony for the PyeongChang 2018 Winter Olympic Games.

3D printing and additive manufacturing

These cover a range of processes and technologies that produce physical objects layer-by-layer from a digital three-dimensional (3D) model. According to ABC News[114], this development could have a bigger impact on economies and society than the internet. Industry analysts believe we are only at the very beginning of understanding the potential of these technologies. Originally, 3D printing was used for rapid prototyping as a means of fast-tracking and reducing the costs of product development, but it is now being considered for much broader applications.

According to McKinsey[115], the economic implications of 3D printing are significant, estimated to be up to US$100–250 billion a year by 2025, mostly from the aerospace and defence, automotive, medical and consumer goods sectors.

This technology allows for new ways of distributed, customisable manufacturing. For example, the technology has the potential to bring the production process closer to its destination, or directly to its customer—eliminating the logistics and supply chain costs associated with mass production. The distributed nature of the technology reduces production risks with smaller batch runs. These have significant impacts on global economies through shifting from production and distribution models to more localised on-demand models, which will reduce imbalances in imports and exports between developing and developed nations.

Some of the industries benefiting from this technology include:

- *Medical and dental*—customisation and personalisation to meet medical standards for items such as hip and knee implants, dental crowns and prosthetics. Although possibly decades away, the technology is being researched and developed for printing skin, bone, tissue and human organs.
- *Aerospace*—companies such as GE/Morris Technologies, Airbus/EADS, Rolls-Royce, BAE Systems and Boeing have been using the technology in their research and developments.
- *Automotive*—prototyping high-performance equipment in motor racing through to prototyping for mass-produced vehicles. This is evolving into the production of on-demand spare/replacement parts, as opposed to holding inventory.
- *Jewellery*—reducing the reliance on high levels of expertise in the manufacturing process, such as fabrication, mould making, casting, electroplating, forging, silver/goldsmithing, stone cutting, engraving and polishing.
- *Architecture*—prototyping models of building or engineering designs with some visionary architects looking at direct construction methods.

Research and development is now underway on four-dimensional (4D) technology that would allow self-altering products capable of adapting to environmental changes.

Advanced robotics

The PyeongChang 2018 Winter Olympics wasn't just for athletes (or drones, for that matter). Robots had their own downhill race and 85 other robots were used to serve drinks, clean floors, swim around fish tanks, and guide visitors at the airport. Standing over 50 centimetres (20 inches) tall, having independent power systems, the ability to stand on two legs and have bendable knees and elbows, eight teams from universities, institutes and private companies competed in a robotic skiing competition at Welli Hilli Park ski resort for the US$10,000 prize.

What South Korea showcased during the games are the extensive applications of advanced robotic technology beyond those that are task-specific. Cobots (a new generation of robots) are now becoming adaptive, flexible and functional, enabling interaction and collaboration between humans, machines and the environment to be a reality. AI enables decisions to be made independently and task performance to adapt to changing conditions. There are many industry examples where research and development of this technology is rapidly progressing. In medical R&D, blood nanobot development is able to imitate human blood cells, fighting diseases and bacteria, and will eventually be capable of delivering chemotherapy that is a thousand times as potent as current methods but without as many side effects.

Oh, did I mention that the winning robot for the world's first Ski Robot Challenge was the 125-centimetre (50-inch) tall, 43-kilogram (95-lb) Taekwon V, built by Minirobot Corporation. Congratulations.

New materials

New materials are emerging that are lighter, stronger, recyclable, conductive, transparent and adaptive. For example: bio-inspired plastic that is light enough to permit flight and thin enough to accommodate flexibility; ultrathin platinum-hydrogen fuel cell vehicles that could provide clean transportation in the future; Graphene, with its strong, conductive, flexible properties, could be applied to next-generation electronic devices, or even sewn into our clothing; and Stanene, which was created as a topological insulator and scientists say is the natural successor to copper interconnects in computers.

Biological

The potential for saving lives is one of the most exciting developments of the Fourth Industrial Revolution. Technology breakthroughs over the part 15 years have significantly reduced scientific research and development costs. Along with increased computing power, data intelligence through AI will make highly-targeted therapies possible, improving quality of life. These breakthroughs have paved the way for next-generation scientific innovations in a range of new areas such as genetic sequencing and gene editing. Synthetic biology, an emerging area of research that enables the design and construction of novel artificial biological pathways, organisms or devices, or the redesign of existing natural biological systems, opens up new ways of thinking about medicine and agriculture.

However, there are also some very significant ethical, social and legal questions that need to be addressed and regulated.

These will challenge our notion of what it means to be human, what information about our bodies such as DNA should be shared, and what rights people have over genetics and their modification. The ability to edit and modify biology (plant, animal and human organisms) provides new ways of thinking about food production, disease management and medicine. While academics, scientists, institutions, governments and communities work through those issues, we will explore the possibilities and advances in biotechnologies, neurotechnologies and brain science, and how they will operate within our own biology and change how we function in the world.

Biotechnologies

For thousands of years, humankind has used biotechnology in medicine and agriculture. We use living systems and living organisms to make and modify products or processes in the areas of bioengineering, biomedical engineering, biomanufacturing and molecular engineering.

There are three main industries where biotechnology offers major possibilities: medical healthcare; agricultural crop production; and non-food uses of crops, such as biofuels, biomaterials and vegetable oils. Examples of applications include:

- *Medical healthcare*—precision medicine that relies upon complex data on the patient's molecular make-up and genomic, transcriptomic, proteomic, metabolic and microbiomic profiles to deliver customised therapies.

- *Agriculture*—food security to meet the global demands for food, its quality and healthcare. Gene editing offers precision crop improvement.
- *Bio refineries*—creating biofuels by using renewable feedstocks that exploit catalytic properties of microorganisms and repurpose CO_2.

The efficiency of biotechnology research that leverages the convergence of biotechnologies with digital technologies is vastly improved with the computational power, machine-learning capabilities and platforms that add intelligence to vast amounts of data. This improves our capacity to design, test and deploy precision solutions to problems that have previously been out of reach.

Neurotechnologies

Neurotechnologies help us understand the brain and how to influence consciousness, thought and higher-order brain activities. While developments with brain imaging have revolutionised the field, other developments include decoding what we are thinking through to new chemicals that influence our brain. New technologies are enabling the measurement, analysis, translation and visualisation of the chemical and electrical signals in the brain. They offer opportunities to address current neurological conditions and physical disabilities. It is anticipated that these technologies will lead to new medical breakthroughs in areas such as:

- *Reading and writing to the brain*—offering the ability to correct deficiencies or add enhancements, such as thought access and influence.
- *Enabling new forms of cognitive computing*—increased knowledge on brain functioning could improve the design of machine-learning algorithms.
- *Perception*—influencing the brain in more precise ways, for example, our sense of self and what constitutes reality.

Neurological disorders impact people the world over economically and socially. These new technologies will improve our ability to diagnose, treat and prevent illnesses such as Alzheimer's and Parkinson's diseases, depression and anxiety—also improving the quality of life for those impacted by those illnesses. They also offer economic benefits through improved individual productivity, personalised education, knowledge and learning.

Virtual, augmented and mixed realities

Virtual, augmented and mixed realities are versions of highly-immersive, audio-visual technologies. Developments in computer processing, visual display and wireless technology are opening up major advances in their applications. While virtual reality, three-dimensional, multisensory technologies can be interacted with in an immersive and seemingly real way using equipment, augmented reality technologies are live, direct or indirect views of a physical, real-world environment. It is the materialisation of what we imagine or want to experience.

Those elements are augmented by computer-generated sensory input, such as sound, video, graphics, etc. Mixed reality brings layers of data information and virtual objects into the environment. These technologies are revolutionising how we interact with the world, creating experiences that are ordinarily out of reach for many people.

These technologies are opening up the imagination economy as their platforms and services create value, offering a completely new channel for consuming experiences and content from anywhere in the world. Advances in neurotechnology and nanotechnology could enable virtual reality to be controlled by our thoughts. Virtual retinal displays, light field displays, and holographic computing represent the next generation of interaction technologies, changing the way humans and computers interact using voice, gesture, physical motion or eye movement. While the applications are endless, here are some practical examples:

- *Education* — across all learning and training environments (e.g. classroom, field training/simulation), enabling collaborative, immersive, anywhere, anytime knowledge experiences.
- *Remote experts* — distributed expertise from specialist healthcare, to field services technicians, to advisory or professional services.
- *Entertainment* — gaming participation, immersive three-dimensional movie experiences.

Expanding the use of these technologies beyond physical environments into mobile environments, such as the early Google Glass product, will come with practical, technical, social and privacy challenges. These are not insurmountable.

Environment

Energy capture, storage and transmission

The energy industry is now entering another industrial revolution, with advances in clean energy and storage and distribution technologies and the global momentum to bring them into commercial operations. As well as the economic benefits of reduced energy costs, most countries recognise the associated environmental benefits and are developing policies to support their expansion into consumer and industrial markets.

Our dependency on fossil fuels to power the world is predicted to become a significant global issue—particularly as our populations increase and the concentrations of those populations have inadequate energy infrastructure. Investment in renewable energy technologies had significantly increased to US$226 billion in 2016[116] and for the first time, renewable energy represented 50 per cent of new power production.

Energy storage research investment continues with both consumer and commercial developments. Smart energy consumption reduces energy costs in consumer markets by discharging during peak demand, shifting energy consumption from one point in time to another and avoiding peak energy pricing. In commercial markets, in addition to those mentioned in the consumer markets, smart energy provides back-up power to avoid outages.

In 2017, the South Australian Government invested in a world first (and largest) Tesla 100W lithium-ion battery after blackouts impacted consumers and businesses that year. Premier Jay Weatherill said: 'the project would fall well within the AU$150 million [the state] set aside for renewable energy alternatives'[117].

Geoengineering

Geoengineering is the notion of large-scale intervention and manipulation of an environmental process that impacts the earth's natural climate systems to counteract the effects of global warming. Techniques include solar radiation management, carbon dioxide removal and stratospheric sulphate aerosols geoengineering. Scientists view that research in these areas are fraught with significant consequences, and as such it is very immature; because it is relatively new, it has received limited research funding. Geoengineering can also be considered in relation to human colonisation of other planets.

Space technologies

Space technologies are developed for use in space exploration, including spacecraft, satellites, space stations and supporting equipment and infrastructure. Commercial developments such as SpaceX have significantly reduced the launch costs. Other developments include exploring enabling aircraft to fly in low earth orbit without landing strips and facilities. Richard Branson has also been looking at space tourism. Along with better access to space, new industries will emerge to support this rapidly developing ecosystem. Advancements in computing, robotics, AI and renewable energy will all play a significant role in improving the economics of space technologies.

Satellites have played an invaluable role in the provision of global connectivity for communication services, provision of location services, the monitoring of the earth's climate and surveillance. The result has been the lowering of barriers for services that today many of us take for granted.

Today, more than 70 countries have operated a satellite in orbit. There are an estimated 1,740 satellites in orbit today and approximately 2,600 decommissioned satellites floating in space, with around 12,000 new satellites to be launched over the next decade[118]. While these space technologies have grown to become a very significant industry, there are still many challenges in expanding into other areas of space development. For example, reducing congestion as more satellites orbit the earth, managing debris, and sharing spectrum frequencies. Public/private partnerships are now unfolding innovation in many new aspects of space technologies and will be critical to its ongoing development.

In summary, the Fourth Industrial Revolution will impact every nation, economy and society. We have much to look forward to—improved health, education, lifestyles and new businesses and industries. The speed and scale of this revolution will be unlike any other because of the significant advancements of the technology revolution, and the willingness of societies to tackle past problems and unexplored horizons. We have much work to do, work that must be done collaboratively so that it benefits all humanity, with collective leadership of both public and private sectors.

The World Economic Forum calls this 'systems leadership', described as cultivating a shared vision for change, collaborating with all stakeholders of a global society, and executing to garner systems benefits. Systems leadership is not targeted at governments or business leaders, but is a paradigm that empowers all citizens and organisations to invest, innovate and deliver value.

We must develop a comprehensive and globally shared view of how technology is affecting our lives and reshaping our economic, social, cultural and human environments. There has never been a time of greater promise, or greater peril.

— Klaus Schwab
founder and executive chairman, World Economic Forum

Chapter summary

- Nations and organisations are yet to fully capitalise on the Third Industrial Revolution and are significantly under-prepared for the fourth in areas of social impact, strategy, talent and technology.

- On the one hand, executives believe overwhelmingly (87 per cent) that the private sector will have the most influence in how this revolution will shape society; yet the same optimism was not reflected in their attitude towards their own organisations (24 per cent).

- When it comes to workforces, 86 per cent of executives reported that they are doing everything possible to create a better workforce for this revolution, but less than a quarter are highly confident they have the right workforce composition and skills for it.

- While this revolution builds on the digital revolution, it will be unlike all others in terms of its speed, impact and scale. It will be a cyber-physical system characterised by new technologies that are merging the physical, digital and biological worlds, predicted to impact all disciplines, economies and industries globally.

- This revolution is expected to also witness emerging breakthrough technologies in the areas of AI, robotics, the IoT, autonomous vehicles, blockchain, 3D printing, quantum computing and nanotechnology.

- Along with the excitement offered by these emerging technologies, there are some very significant ethical, social and legal issues to be addressed and regulated.

CONCLUSION

Well, Youthquake has arrived—again. What is similar between the mid-1960s version and now is how quickly each generation's cultural, social and political influence unfolded globally. What is different is that the combined impact of demographic change, the trust crisis we find ourselves in today, and the promises of emerging technologies, will be of meteoritic proportions—and so our capacity to adapt must also be of that proportion.

The Millennial generation has a new explanation for cultural, political and social change. Tapping into their enormous capacity to see the world through a different lens and their distinct vision for the future is one of the most enduring qualities for society as a whole.

Millennials have grown up in a world that is their neighborhood, unconstrained by geography but characterised by instability, which has led them to develop a general sense of distrust. We have already seen what happens when they throw their democratic power behind political groups. We've seen what happens when they throw their economic power behind brands that are socially and environmentally conscious. We've seen what happens when their consumption-based preferences shift toward subscription-based services, and how this threatens traditional models still based on ownership. And we've seen what happens when their silence disrupts organisations and institutions they've lost faith in.

Capitalising on the significant representation of Millennials in a population could return to that nation a demographic dividend that leads to economic growth. However, the challenge for today's leaders is to set a course that will unlock the potential of this remarkable generation.

Millennials need to be heard and we need to understand that their views are not at the expense of other demographic groups. They know all too well the challenges faced by all members of society, particular on matters of diversity and sustainability. However, unlike other generations, empowerment is their oxygen, and they've got plenty of it.

Trust is in crisis, but we simply can't fix it with yesterday's logic. Despite the failings of the existing trust model, it can be adapted and changed to fit with our digital society. Trust is the most important renewable energy of our technological evolution.

The conditions upon which we trust people, ideas and platforms—the trust trinity—have profoundly shifted away from a hierarchical-based, vertical model, concentrated in the hands of institutions in which we've lost faith, in favour of a democratised, horizontal-based model that distributes trust among communities at a global scale, with real-time speed and a symmetrical impact.

Technology and machines are also founded on trust and reputation, particularly in light of the tsunami of robotic, autonomous vehicles, monitoring equipment, sensors, and objects in development and use. Interconnected, distributed trust will fuse the physical, digital and biological worlds, requiring a paradigm shift in relationships between people and technology. This is another reason why the Fourth Industrial Revolution differs from those in the past. Trust leaps will be critical in opening up the horizons and opportunities of the Fourth Industrial Revolution, by unlocking the human capital of our Millennial generation to create, innovate and take the required risks on the world's behalf.

The history of the labour market demonstrates how well human capital has adapted over the past three industrial revolutions. As we enter the next revolution, our priority must be in ensuring the equilibrium of the new skills required, and the rebalancing of existing skills. However, the speed, scale and impact of this next revolution, particularly in knowledge-based sectors, requires a level of adaptability and agility that can only be achieved with much greater collaboration between governments, educational institutions and organisations.

It requires resolving the single most important human capital issue of our time—diversity. How can we claim we've optimised all that the Third Industrial Revolution had to offer when the evidence suggests that, globally, a third of companies have no women in either board or C-suite positions—when we know that organisations with 30 per cent female leaders can add up to six per cent in net margin? Gender diversity has the potential to add between US$12–28 trillion, or 11–26 per cent of global GDP by 2025. We've seen Millennials make socially-conscious investment choices in asset classes. It's only a matter of time before they start making investment choices based on an organisation's diversity performance. Why? Because the more diverse an organisation, the better it performs. Simple as that.

Millennials now make up half of all workers in many countries, and this will only increase over time. This demographic simply won't tolerate workplaces that don't reflect the equality standards they expect. Their confidence in business has declined, their desire for greater flexibility in the workplace and a positive work culture has increased and, most disturbingly, they are feeling unprepared for the changing nature of work. The underlying causes of this are due to a mismatch of priorities and an overwhelming feeling by Millennials that business success should be measured beyond financial performance. Millennials believe organisations should prioritise making a positive impact on society, creating innovative products, services, jobs, career development and improving people's lives.

Purpose, inclusion and diversity are critical to Millennials, not only for alignment of values, but because they see what they do in life as being intertwined with who they are. They will be very willing to look beyond their home country in pursuit of that. With this demographic, competition for human capital is no longer a domestic issue, but a global one.

Longevity is another issue to consider. Life expectancy has been steadily increasing by two years each decade since 1840. A Millennial aged 20 has a 50 per cent chance of living to 100 years or more. Time—the scarcest resource—has now become more abundant for Millennials than any other generation, and we need to consider how longevity will impact society, economies, businesses and industries.

The three-stage model of education, employment and retirement is outdated and simply won't accommodate Millennials' longer lives, or those of the generations that follow. Juvenescence—the state of youthfulness—is more aligned to how Millennials will allocate this surplus time, by shifting away from age-related life stages to age-agnostic stages. Recreation with these age-agnostic life stages requires investment in shifting identities to take on new roles, different lifestyles or the development of new skills. To Millennials living a 100-year life, creative success needs to be redesigned to shift the model to individual fulfilment through self-actualisation.

A performance gap has now emerged between those organisations that invested in digital transformations and are applying digital technologies and strategies, and those that are still competing in traditional ways. Without digitisation, a third of revenues are predicted to be at risk of loss or cannibalization in the next three years; but those organisations that are adopting digitisation and hold significant market share are just as great a threat to digital laggards.

The concentration of digitisation at an industry level results in declining profit and revenue pools. Digital leaders and innovators exhibit common characteristics, such as innovating their business models in a transformational way, scaling up cutting-edge technologies and techniques. They apply design thinking at scale across the organisation or within business units; they invest decisively and three times as much, and for the long term relative to traditional companies; and they see the world as interconnected ecosystems.

What holds organisations back from transforming is the irreconcilable economic, strategic and operational differences between their business-as-usual traditional model and the pace and scale of the disruptive transformational models around them.

Organisations have now emerged that leverage the power of platform-based, data-intensive and capital-light models designed with exponential technologies that scale for exponential performance. Disruptive organisations restructure value chains by taking what was once physical in nature and dematerialising it into the digital, on-demand world, disaggregating inefficient and costly processes, separating them into frictionless components, and disintermediating by cutting out the non value-adding middleman. They now pose existential threats to many organisations and the traditional industry structures.

As the information enablement of industries, products and services accelerates, there has never been a more important time for traditional, linear-based model organisations to consider their economic and human capital investments to transform and compete in an exponential world. The dematerialisation, demonetisation and democratisation of technologies will put powerful tools in the hands of individuals, where in the past they were reserved for major corporations. But despite 52 per cent of large public companies in Europe and North America announcing transformations in 2016—a 42 per cent increase since 2006—the results have not followed.

When considering growth of the total shareholder return (TSR) of transforming companies relative to that of their respective industry, only 24 per cent experienced greater TSG growth over both the short term (one year), and the long term (five years-plus).

Data has now become the digital lifeblood for how we live and run our businesses, economies and governments. For organisations in this age of transformation, data has become the currency that allows them to compete analytically. One of the most important emerging technologies using data is AI, which could drive GDP gains of US$15.7 trillion with productivity and personalisation improvements. The greatest economic advances in AI will be in China (26 per cent growth in GDP by 2030) and North America (14.5 per cent growth)—the equivalent of US$10.7 trillion. These countries are in an AI race.

The Fourth Industrial Revolution will be a cyber-physical system characterised by new technologies that are merging the physical, digital and biological worlds, and predicted to impact all disciplines, economies and industries globally. This revolution is also expected to witness emerging breakthrough technologies in the areas of AI, robotics, the IoT, autonomous vehicles, blockchain, 3D printing, quantum computing and nanotechnology.

These technological breakthroughs give us optimism and we have much to look forward to—improved health, education, lifestyles and new businesses and industries. The speed, scale and impact of this revolution will be unlike any other, due to the significant advancements of the technology revolution, and the willingness of societies to tackle the unresolved problems and unexplored horizons of the past.

The World Economic Forum is calling for systems leadership through cultivating a shared vision for change, collaborating with all stakeholders of a global society, and executing to garner system benefits limited only by our imaginations and the brilliance of our human capital.

Let's not forget that every invention or innovation, whether the steam engine from the First Industrial Revolution, telecommunications from the Second Industrial Revolution, or a computer or smartphone from the Third Industrial Revolution, began as an idea in someone's mind. The world we know today was designed and built as an extension of our imaginations—so let's begin imagining the Fourth Industrial Revolution.

I hope this book has helped bring out the juvenescence in you. My heart is filled with joy by the thought that in my lifetime I will witness this Millennial generation taking leadership of the world. I'm also grateful that my children will grow up in a world led by Millennials, bringing to life the advancements that the Fourth Industrial Revolution offers. I also hope this book has bought happiness and hope to you as it has for me.

I started this book with a wonderful quote from John F. Kennedy about how future promise can be measured by the prospects of its youth, and I'll finish this book with another wonderful quote from him. I hope it empowers you to think about change and what role you want it to play in adapting your life, as it has for mine.

Change is the law of life and those who look only to the past or present are certain to miss the future.

— **John F. Kennedy**
35th President of the United States

NOTES

1   Based on US Census Bureau data, January 2018

2   Gratton, L and Scott A., *The 100-Year Life: Living and Working in an Age of Longevity* (Bloomsbury, 2016)

3   World Economic Forum (January 2017), 'These are the most fragile cities in the world—and this is what we've learned from them'

4   United Nations (2014), 'World Urbanisation Prospects 2014'

5   McAfee, A, Brynjolfsson, E, *Machine, Platform, Crowd: Harnessing Our Digital Future*; New York (Norton & Company, 2017)

6   IDC, Intel, United Nations, 'A Guide to the Internet of things Infographic' www.intel. com (accessed 19 February 2018)

7   Defined as an economy where intuitive and creative thinking create economic value, after logical and rational thinking has been outsourced to other economies.

8   World Economic Forum, (2016), 'The fourth Industrial Revolution: what it means, how to respond'

9   Oxford Dictionary (2017), 'Word of the Year 2017 is….'

10 *Vanity Fair* (2017), 'How a 52-Year-Old Word Invented by a Vogue Editor Became 2017's Word of the Year'

11 McKenzie, Scott (1967), 'San Francisco (Be Sure to Wear Flowers in Your Hair)'. Writers: John Edmund, Andrew Phillips; Publishers Universal Music Group 1967

12 OECD, Education Attainment – Population with Tertiary Education – OECD Data

13 Bank of America Merrill Lynch (July 2015), 'Thematic Investing Generation Next – Millennials Primer'

14 Schwab, Klaus. *The Fourth Industrial Revolution* (Crown Publishing Group, 2016)

15 Pricewaterhouse Coopers and CB Insights (2017), '2017 Money Tree Report'

16 BBC News Magazine, (24 June 2016), 'Brexit: How much of a generation gap is there?'

17 United Nations, (2015), 'World Population Aging'

18 Bank of America Merrill Lynch (July 2015), 'Thematic Investing Generation Next— Millennials Primer'

19 AT Kearney (July 2016), 'Where are the Global Millennials'

20 United Nations, (2015), 'World Population Aging'

21 World Economic Forum (2017), 'Global Shapers Annual Survey 2017' '#ShapersSurvey'

22 Bank of America Merrill Lynch (December 2016), 'Theme Watch. YA 2017: Year of Tech Disruption, Earth & Millennials Themes'

23 Accenture (6 September 2016), 'Retailers and Consumer Packaged Goods Companies Must Enhance Their Understanding of Millennial Consumers to Capture Share of $6 Trillion Wallet in Asia'

24 Boston Consulting Group (2016), 'Global Wealth Market Sizing Database, 2016 – BCG Analysis'

25 CB Insights (November 2017), 'Acorns Teardown: The most popular Robo-Advisor faces a fierce fight as it goes "upmarket"'

26 CB Insights (March 2018), 'Millennials are Driving one of the Biggest Trends in Wealth Tech'

27 Yale University (May 2017), 'Student Debt Rising Worldwide'

28 *Sydney Morning Herald* (February 2016), 'Young people saddled by a higher degree of debt'

29 Federal Reserve Bank (2015), 'Report on the Economic Well-Being of US Households in 2015

30 Digital Marketing Business (2017), 'Chinese Millennials on their mobiles'

31 Pew Research Centre, (2017) '10 demographic trends shaping the US and the world in 2017'

32 Neilson (2016), 'Millennials are top smartphone uses'

33 The Financial Brand (2017), 'The rise of the digital only banking customer'

34 Business Insider (July 2017), 'This chart reveals a huge difference in how US Millennials and their parents spend money'

35 Experian (January 2017), 'State of Credit: 2017'

36 TSYS (2016), 'Addressing Generational Shifts Among Cardholders'

37 UBS (June 2017). 'Millennials—the global guardians of Capital', UBS Chief Investment Office Wealth Management white paper

38 Deloitte (2017), 'Millennials and wealth management. Trends and challenges of the new clientele'

39 Governance Studies at Brookings Report (2014), 'How Millennials Could Upend Wall Street and Corporate America'

40 Deloitte (2018), 'The 2018 Deloitte Millennial Survey'

41 Deloitte (2017), 'The 2017 Deloitte Millennial Survey'

42 World Economic Forum (2017), 'The Global Human Capital Report 2017—Preparing people for the future of work'

43 Korn Ferry Institute (2016), 'The trillion-dollar difference'

44 Finextra (2015), 'Gates makes mobile banking bet'

45 GSMA (2017), 'Mobile Economy 2017'

46 Hootsuite (January 2018), 'Digital Around the World in 2018'

47 Brookings (November 2016), 'The Internet as a human right'

48 McCrindle, Mark and Wolfinger, Emily, *The ABC of XYZ: Understanding the Global Generations* (University of New South Wales Press, 2009)

49 App Annie (2017), 'The App Economy Forecast: $6 Trillion in New Value'

50 GSMA (February 2018), 'Consumer Insights: Understanding mobile Engagement'

51 Ericsson (November 2017), 'Millennials Expectations for 5G'

52   Ericsson and Vodafone (2016), 'Content in the Blink of an Eye,' Using neuroscience to understand the impact of varying network performance on smartphone users

53   Hootsuite (January 2018), 'Digital Around the World in 2018'

54   Botsman, R. *Who Can You Trust? How Technology Brought Us Together and Why It Might Drive Us Apart* (Public Affairs New York, 2017)

55   Edelman (2017), '2017 Edelman Trust Barometer'

56   The Trust-building Attributes include integrity, engagement, products, purpose and operations. Additional Dimensions that Inform Business Trust include employee empowerment, diversity, citizenship, leadership and relationship building.

57   Gemalto (2017), 'Poor Internal Security Practices Take a Toll, Findings from the first half 2017 Breach Level Index'

58   Bloomberg (2016), Kaplan, J. 'The Inventor of Customer Satisfaction Surveys is Sick of Them'

59   Botsman, R. *Who Can You Trust? How Technology Brought Us Together and Why It Might Drive Us Apart* (Public Affairs New York, 2017)

60   CISCO (2016), 'The next generation of the Internet is coming with Blockchain'

61   Stiglitz, J. (2013), 'In No One We Trust'

62   McKinsey & Company (November 2017), 'What the future of work will mean for jobs, skills and wages'

63   GTCI (2018), 'Talent diversity to fuel the future of work'

64   McKinsey Global Institute (2015), 'The Power of Parity: How advancing women's equality can add $12 trillion to global growth'

65   The Peterson Institute for International Economics & EY (2016), 'Is Gender Diversity Profitable? Evidence from a Global Study'

66   Australian Government (November 2017), 'Australia's gender equality scorecard 2016–17'

67   Deloitte (2017), 'Diversity and Inclusion: The reality gap'

68   Garr, A. and Mallon, 'High impact talent management'

69   Perkins, M. (2016), *The Age*, 'Victorian Government trials blind job applications to overcome hiring bias'

70   ABC News' The Business Presenter (March 2018), 'Energy Australia closes gender pay gap overnight, literally'

71   Deloitte (2015), 'The Radical transformation of Diversity and Inclusion—The Millennial Influence'

72   Resolution Foundation (February 2018), 'Intergenerational Commission Report; Cross Countries, International comparisons of intergenerational trends'

73   Deaton, A. *The Great Escape: Health, Wealth and the Origins of Inequality* (Princeton University Press, 2013)

74   Gratton, L & Scott, A. *The 100 Year Life: Living and Working in an Age of Longevity* (2017)

75   Stanford Centre on Longevity, (2017), 'Shifting Life Milestones across Ages: a Matter of Preference or Circumstance?'

76   Foster, R. Yale University; Babson Olin Graduate School of Business, 2011

77   OECD (November 2017) 'Health at a Glance—OECD Indicators'

78   Productivity Commission and Melbourne Institute of Applied Economic and Social Research 1999, 'Policy Implications of the Ageing of Australia's Population' Conference Proceedings, AusInfo, Canberra

79 OECD (2013), 'Trends Shaping Education – Spotlight 1: Aging Societies'

80 https://www.youtube.com/watch?v=dgf0OUsQJuA&sns=em

81 *The Independent* (March 2018), 'More than half of Millennials going through 'quarter-life' crisis, research finds'

82 Business Insider Australia (March 2018), 'Australia's millennials are having a "quarter life crisis" as they worry about being successful'

83 Wolverson, R. (2013), 'The Best Age for a Start-Up Founder', Time Magazine

84 McKinsey & Company (October 2016), 'Independent Work: Choice, Necessity, and the Gig Economy'

85 McKinsey & Company (October 2017), 'How digital reinventors are pulling away from the pack'

86 McKinsey & Company (January 2018), 'Why digital strategies fail'

87 BCG (January 2018), 'The CFO's Vital Role in Corporate Transformation'

88 Ismal, S., Malone, M. and Geest, Y. *Exponential Organisations* (Diversion Books, 2014)

89 Statista (2018), 'Digital Economy Compass'

90 Kurswell, R. (2006) 'The Singularity is Near' (Penguin Publishing)

91 Visual Capitalist, (December 2017), 'The 57 Start-ups That Became Unicorns in 2017'

92 http://f100.exponentialorgs.com/ Accessed on 27 January 2018

93 Information Age (February 2017), 'Digital disruption will wipe out 40 per cent of Fortune 500 firms in next 10 years, say c-suite execs'

94 CB Insights (November 2017), 'On Earnings Calls, Which Tech Company Are Senior Execs Most Obsessed With? Hint: It's No Longer Google' https://app.cbinsights.com/research/amazon-apple-google-earnings-call-transcripts/

95 McKinsey & Company (December 2017), 'Digital China: Powering the Economy to Global Competitiveness'

96 Market Realist (January 2018), 'Why Mobile Payments Have dethroned Cash as King in China'

97 New York Times (July 20, 2017), 'Beijing Wants A.I. to be Made in China by 2030'

98 Davenport, H and Harris, J, (2007), *Competing on analytics—The New Science of Winning* (Harvard Business School Press)

99 IDC (April 2017), 'Data Age 2025: The Evolution of Data to Life-Critical'

100 Deloitte (February 2017), 'Dark analytics: Illuminating opportunities hidden within unstructured data'

101 Accenture Analytic (2016), 'The 5As of Analytics Transformation: Embedding analytics DNA into business decision making'

102 *Sydney Morning Herald* (January 18, 2018), 'Drone used to save two swimmers caught in rough surf at Lennox Head'

103 PWC (2017), 'Sizing the prize—what's the real value of AI for your business and how can you capitalise?'

104 McKinsey & Company, (April 2018), 'Notes from the AI frontier: Applications and value of deep learning'

105 KPMG International (July 2017), 'Guardians of trust — who Is responsible for trusted analytics in the digital age?'

106 Deloitte Global and Forbes Insights (January 2018), 'The Fourth Industrial Revolution is here—are you ready?'

107 Schwab, K. and David, N. World Economic Forum (2018), *Shaping the Fourth Industrial Revolution*

108 IBM, 'Quantum computing applications', IBM Q–US www.research.ibm.com accessed on 15 February 2018

109 McKinsey & Company (January 2017), 'Blockchain Technology in the Insurance Sector'

110 Statista, 'Size of the Internet of Things worldwide in 2014 and 2020, by industry (in billion U.S. dollars)'

111 GrowthEnabler (2017), 'Market Pulse Report, Internet of Things'

112 World Economic Forum and Accenture (2016), 'The Internet of Things and connected devices: making the world smarter' (Geneva: World Economic Forum)

113 McKinsey Global Institute (2015), 'Internet of Things: Mapping the Value Beyond the Hype'

114 ABC News (April 2015), '3D printing will have a bigger economic impact than the internet, technology specialists say'

115 McKinsey & Company (September 2017), 'Additive manufacturing: A long-term game changer for manufacturers'

116 Frankfurt School of Finance & Management (2017), 'Global Trends in Renewable Energy Investment'

117 Amp.com.au (July 2017), 'Everything you need to know about Tesla's battery in South Australia'

118 *Business Insider* (2018), 'Elon Musk is about to launch the first of 11,925 proposed SpaceX internet satellites—more than all spacecraft that orbit the earth today'

ABOUT THE AUTHOR

 Rocky Scopelliti is a world-renowned futurologist. His pioneering research on the confluence of demographic change associated with Millennials and digital technology has influenced the way we think about our social, cultural, economic and technological future.

As a media commentator, his unique insights have featured on Sky Business News, *The Australian Financial Review*, ABC Radio National, *The Economist*, Forbes and Bloomberg. As an international keynote speaker, his presentations have informed audiences across the Asia Pacific, the United States and Europe, including Mobile World Congress in Barcelona. As a thought leader, each year over 150 boards and leadership teams, including Fortune 100 corporations, seek his advice on strategy.

A distinguished author, his 12 published thought leadership research reports have become internationally recognised for their influence, including by the World Economic Forum's Disruptive Innovation in Financial Services Program.

In an executive capacity, he is a member of the Optus Business Leadership team as the Director Centre for Industry 4.0, where he leads a specialist team creating world-class thought leadership and innovation on the Fourth Industrial Revolution.

He is a director on the board of Community First Credit Union in a non-executive capacity.

Educated in Australia and the United States at Sydney and Stanford universities, he has a Graduate Diploma in Corporate Management and an MBA. He is also a graduate and member of the Australian Institute of Company Directors.